FINDING
YOUR WAY
THROUGH
DEPRESSION

Other Books by Pam Rosewell Moore:

Life Lessons from the Hiding Place

With her husband, Carey Moore:
If Two Shall Agree, later published as *What Happens When Husbands and Wives Pray Together?*

FINDING YOUR WAY THROUGH DEPRESSION

PAM ROSEWELL MOORE

SPIRE

© 2000 by Pam Rosewell Moore

Published by Fleming H. Revell
a division of Baker Publishing Group
P.O. Box 6287, Grand Rapids, MI 49516-6287

Spire edition published 2005

Second printing, February 2006

ISBN 10: 0-8007-8726-9
ISBN 978-0-8007-8726-4

Previously published under the title When Spring Comes Late by Chosen Books

Printed in the United States of America

Permission to quote "Weightlifting" by Michael Williams in chapter-10 is gratefully acknowledged. Copyright © 1992 by Michael Williams.

Unless otherwise marked, all Scripture is taken from the HOLY BIBLE, NEW INTERNATIONAL VERSION®. NIV®. Copyright © 1973, 1978, 1984 by International Bible Society. Used by permission of Zondervan. All rights reserved.

Scripture marked KJV is taken from the King James Version of the Bible.

Scripture marked NKJV is taken from the New King James Version. Copyright ©1982 by Thomas Nelson, Inc. Used by permission. All rights reserved.

Scripture marked RSV is taken from the Revised Standard Version of the Bible, copyright 1952 [2nd edition, 1971] by the Division of Christian Education of the National Council of the Churches of Christ in the United States of America. Used by permission. All rights reserved.

for Deana Hancock Adams

Contents

Acknowledgments

In my search for a compassionate Christian view of clinical depression, I have been helped by hundreds of women and men who know what it is by experience, and who have allowed me to inquire about their own questions and conclusions. With much respect, I thank them.

And I extend grateful appreciation to my patient editor and friend, Jane Campbell.

Introduction

It was my first visit to Nebraska, and two members of the committee that had invited me to speak to the women's fall retreat of their church met me at the airport at Omaha. The day was clear and bright. Here and there hints of fall color showed up in the palette of varying greens on the tree-filled landscape. Since the journey to the country retreat center would take about an hour, Marybeth, Marlys and I had the opportunity to get to know each other. I liked them immediately.

Marlys, a young mother, was the director of women's ministries at their church. And Marybeth had corresponded with me by e-mail for the past several months as retreat plans developed. A strong-looking and capable young woman, she was the one who had invited me to be speaker at this retreat. Having just married for the first time at 35 years of age, she had bought my book *Safer than a Known Way* at a filling station. She had identified with me as I told, among other things, how in the Lord's will I had waited for marriage until I was 42 years old.

We three gained rapport swiftly, mainly because we had a strong common goal. We all wanted to minister at the weekend retreat in such a way that the women attending would be strengthened, refreshed and brought a step farther in their Christian lives.

"Is it all right with you if, during one session, I talk about the Christian and depression?" I asked Marybeth and Marlys.

I am always careful to ask permission to speak about depression. In some meetings—fewer than in the past, I am glad to say—it is definitely not all right, even though current statistics tell us that one woman in four will struggle with depression at some time in her life. Many men will, too, but since fewer admit it, an estimate of how many is hard to arrive at.

It *was* all right for me to speak about depression. And as we drove that autumn day, my two new friends and I entered a conversation that would dominate half our car journey to the retreat site. I told Marybeth and Marlys that, to my great surprise, my own Christian journey had held a struggle with this problem.

"I've just come back from a meeting of the leaders of women's ministries in our denomination," Marlys said. "One of the questions we asked ourselves was, What is the Church going to do about depression?"

So I brought the subject of the Christian and depression into my talks that weekend. The results in Nebraska were no surprise to me. They were consistent with responses all over the country at retreats and meetings of committed Christian women:

Relief and gratitude from depressed or recovering Christians

A desire to learn about the subject from many well Christians

Caution from those who would rather not yet learn much about the subject

Surprise from a small number of women who had no idea what I was talking about

In the following pages I want to bring my contribution to the discussion of one of the biggest concerns of the Church early in the third millennium. What is the Church, and what are individual Christians, going to do about depression?

But I must emphasize the words *my contribution*. I am an ordinary Christian, no expert in theology or psychology. Even if I were, there is much about depression that remains mysterious, despite helpful neurochemical advances.

Some scientists of our day hold a strongly mechanistic approach. They almost seem to say that men and women are just heaps of chemicals and that if the right medicines are taken, depression can be cured. Would that approach not also seem to say that the symptoms and behaviors of depression are never the depressed person's fault? That responses are chemically determined?

At the other end of the debate are Christians (many formally trained in theology) who say that antidepressant medication is never the answer for the Christian. The depressed person's symptoms and behavior should be rectified by the correct application of faith. Lack of healing implies lack of faith.

Having met both these views in my own case of clinical depression, I have many questions. What *is* the Church going to do about depression? How can a Christian like me become part of the answer to such a widespread problem? How can I help understanding and love to increase?

Here are some of the issues I have had in mind as I wrote the following pages:

When a person is no longer able to function normally because of depression, it is correctly termed an illness. Illnesses need treating.

What may have led up to an emotional collapse in any particular case? Since everyone is different, and since the circumstances of our lives differ, must we not often say that we do not fully know?

13

Why do some people recover after antidepressant medicine is prescribed? Why do others recover with no medication? What about those who say they have tried every possible medicine and nothing helped? Who knows the answers to these questions? The medical community? The Church?

Why do some people need to continue antidepressant medicine in order to maintain emotional health? Why do other people respond to medication fairly quickly and never need to take it again? Nobody seems to know exactly why.

Since so much is not known, should sweeping generalizations about Christians and depression ever be made by those in the Church? What does the Lord Jesus Christ say to the depressed Christian? How can His healing and comfort be received?

Come with me as we consider these and other questions, and seek to find a way through depression for those to whom spring comes late.

I said to the man who stood at the gate of the year, "Give me a light that I may tread safely into the unknown." And he replied, "Go out into the darkness and put your hand into the hand of God. That shall be to you better than light and safer than a known way!"

So I went forth and, finding the hand of God, trod gladly into the night. And He led me towards the hills and the breaking of day in the lone East.

Minnie Louise Haskins

The Gate of the Year

The sacrifices of God are a broken spirit;
a broken and contrite heart, O God, you
will not despise.

Psalm 51:17

On New Year's Day 1996 my husband, Carey, and I sat in the front room of our house in Grand Prairie, Texas, on two large, dark blue easy chairs, relaxing with cups of coffee. We sat with our backs to the windows facing west, behind which stretched miles of flat prairie land, now under rapid development.

We were glad we could spend some quiet hours together in our comfortable house. I always enjoyed the harmony of its blue carpets and white walls, against which we had placed mementos of our different nationalities and years as marriage partners, as well as of our places of work and travel before we knew each other.

On display were Delft blue plates from the Netherlands, teapots from England,

17

Poland, Hungary and Germany, and a set of arrows from Carey's travels in Brazil. A small blue rack on the wall held souvenirs from his time in high school in Dallas, the Air Force and various places to which his previous work in journalism and editing had led him. Through these reminders we often took mental excursions. I knew there would be time for more imaginative wanderings this January 1. Tomorrow we would return to our busy lives at Dallas Baptist University, where Carey was a librarian and I worked as director of the intercessory prayer ministry. But today we had the day off.

After we married in 1986, when I was 42 years old and Carey ten years my elder, it had been a joy for me to find that he was the same person he appeared to be before the wedding. Optimistic, kind, consistent and laid back, Carey was concerned about preparing for future events as much as possible, but he did not try to anticipate calamities. This attitude gave me much rest, for my own tendency was to imagine the worst in any situation. I was sure that his calm personality, blended with my more intense one, was a big factor in our happiness as a couple. "You always calm me down," I had said to him countless times in the ten years since we had first met in Waco, Texas. We had been introduced by Dorothy Shellenberger and her husband, Charles, long-time residents of Waco. They had become my "adoptive" American parents ten years before when my work had taken me to that city.

I watched Carey finish his cup of coffee. He looked much younger than his 62 years. Even the fact that he had suddenly become bald had not detracted from his good looks, I noted—a thought that had been confirmed just a few days previously.

"Carey looks so handsome without his hair," said Dorothy one day on a visit from Waco. She had not seen him since the treatments had begun.

Carey placed his coffee cup firmly on the saucer and turned toward me. His hazel eyes looked into my brown ones, and he straightened his shoulders.

"Why don't we take some time apart," he said, "and go over the past year in our journals? We can write down some of the things we've seen the Lord do in our lives in 1995. Then this afternoon, after Bob's visit, let's share some of those things, and pray and make plans about our goals for 1996."

Receiving my agreement, the ever-optimistic Carey climbed the stairs to his study at the front of the house.

Carey had made this suggestion on some previous New Year's Days, and although I normally shared his enthusiasm, this time I did not. I stayed in the enveloping and safe dark blue chair, not wanting to get started.

During the past few months I had felt increasingly tired and overwhelmed. Everything seemed to be getting harder to cope with. I was experiencing an ever-present, all-pervading sadness. To turn back the pages of my journal into last year was too difficult a task to face.

Yet 1995 had started happily enough. We had anticipated with considerable joy the June wedding of Carey's son, Jim, then 28 years old. Jim was a chief joy in my life. He had lived with us for several years. The wedding day came and both families celebrated with enthusiasm.

Back in our regular lives, three days later, Carey was driving north from Dallas Baptist University to the University of North Texas in Denton, where he was working on a master's degree in library science. Toward the end of the hour-long journey, for no particular reason, he placed his right hand on his left collarbone and felt a raised swelling in the hollow above.

Since he had not noticed it before, even mellow Carey acted swiftly, making an appointment with our family doctor immediately. Referrals to two specialists followed, a biopsy of two swollen lymph nodes was performed in July, and Carey was diagnosed with a malignancy of unknown origin. The malignant tissue proved to be a secondary and not a primary cancer growth. Radiation and chemotherapy were prescribed. As of this New Year's Day, five months later, Carey had received six weeks of radiation and two chemotherapy treatments. He was going through this with characteristic cheerfulness and optimism.

I wondered how this was possible. Having had a lifelong interest in things medical (probably because of my mother's long nursing career), I knew the seriousness of his diagnosis of cancer of an unknown origin. By the time secondary growths such as these are discovered, the original malignancy may already have affected several vital organs. I had seen this happen to my mother, who passed away in 1983. Carey, I reasoned, did not have more than the average non-professional's interest in medicine. He could not understand how serious this was. If he did, surely he would not be making plans for 1996! He might not live to see more than a few months of the new year.

From the safety of the armchair, I sought for the thousandth time to take myself in hand.

Where is your initiative? I asked myself. *Why don't you get moving?* But I did not feel like my old self at all. I felt as though a new, strange, deeply sad self had taken over. Then it was as if I had a conversation with myself from two perspectives.

"Snap out of this!" said the old Pam.

"I've tried and I can't!" said the sad one.

"You can do all things through Christ who strengthens you," said the old me bluntly, quoting a favorite Bible verse.

"I know and believe that."

"Then why isn't it working?"

"I don't know," said the sad one slowly.

Suddenly the blue armchair did not feel quite as safe. I realized I was about to reenter a pattern of almost constantly circling thoughts. This pattern had somehow entrenched itself in my mind during the last five months and seemed impossible to break out of. I had tried many times, through prayer and through rallying resolve. Nothing worked. If I did not try to break the circling thoughts again now, the neurotic pattern would engulf me and I would still be sitting in the armchair an hour from now, with no resolution. There never was resolution. It seemed hopeless.

Standing up, I climbed the stairs on the way to my little book-filled study at the back of the house. At the top of the stairs I looked over my left shoulder and saw Carey in his study.

Will I still have him next New Year's Day? I asked myself.

There were those death-filled and fearful circling thoughts again! If only I could break out of them. I could see they were unhealthy and obsessive.

Sitting with his back to me at his desk, facing the window, his Bible, prayer list and 1995 daily journal open before him, Carey was intent on his purpose of reviewing the past year. The sensibleness of it cut across my whirling thoughts. After all, Carey was presenting a hopeful and encouraging scene. Armed with those adjectives, I turned down the hall and entered my study.

If Carey can review last year with purpose while he is undergoing chemotherapy, I thought, *surely you can.*

Mustering courage, I picked up my journal for 1995 and began some New Year's Day reflections. As time proceeded and I read descriptions of events in previous months, I was struck not so much by the happenings; they were all too familiar and had made thousands of whirls through my brain. No, it was my attitudes and reactions to the events that caught my attention.

"I am so very tired" sounded with boring frequency from my journal.

"If only I could sleep!" was another complaint, referring to frequent awakenings at three A.M. with no refreshing rest after that hour.

"I am preoccupied with death" referred to what I perceived as Carey's soon-to-be-fatal illness. Although fascination with death was not new to me, having been a close companion

21

since early childhood, the thought of death threatening the dearest person on earth to me was almost unbearable.

I stood up, stretched and remained standing for a while, admiring the still-elegant shapes of the bare limbs of our two willow trees in the small backyard. The thought about to come was most unexpected.

Fatigue, sleeplessness, death . . . why were the words familiar? Then I recalled seeing them several times over past months in articles. They were said to be symptoms of clinical depression.

But you're not depressed, intoned the old Pam briskly, anticipating a tentatively forming question. *Serious Christians cannot be depressed.*

It was my long-held view that depression resulted from a lack of total surrender to God's will.

I heard no sound from Carey's study. How were his ideas on 1995 forming? Surely his were on a completely different track from mine.

Aware of the self-absorbed nature of my thoughts, and annoyed by them, I returned to the chair at my desk, determined to be more objective. I was hindered, however, by the unconnectedness of my diary entries.

What lack of concentration in a person who loves words and tries to use them precisely, I said to myself irritably.

Then came that sense of familiarity again. *Lack of concentration*—was that not on the list of symptoms of depression? Wanting to bury the thought, I continued to read the journal entries. The most painful one recalled a time a few weeks back when I had been angry and irritable with Carey for no reason. That morning, at the very time he needed my calm support as he went through radiation and chemotherapy, I had responded to an inquiry of his with unbridled frustration and a stream of words.

He had merely asked whether the sandwich lunches, which I usually prepared, were ready to take to the car. They were not. My angry response had been uncontrollable. It had frightened me at the time, and it frightened me now as I recalled the incident. No wonder I had not wanted to go back into the past year!

Again came the sense of familiarity: *irritability*. Another symptom.

Other memories crowded in. What about those times when I had begun to weep at work, when I had not been able to control my tears when a prayer request was brought to my office or relayed to me by phone or e-mail? How embarrassing it had been, for instance, when I had wept in the presence of a trustee of the university as I listened to his account of his mother's illness! I had not been able to withhold tears. It had not helped him and it was simply not a normal thing for me to do.

Then the sad me turned away slightly from the old me. Could I be depressed? For the first time I admitted the possibility.

Soon I heard Carey leaving his office and descending the staircase. It was time to eat. I had better make tracks downstairs, too. That afternoon a long-time friend of Carey's, in Texas for a short while, was coming by for a visit.

After lunch Carey built a fire in the fireplace of our cozy sitting room at the back of the house. His friend Bob, a missionary pilot, soon arrived, and the two talked animatedly about previous adventures, as well as the stories Bob had written and Carey had edited for Bob's missions magazines. The old spirit of adventure began to rise in me as I listened, and I welcomed it. The three of us sipped tea together in front of the fire. The circling thoughts had gone for a while, and life felt almost normal.

But after Bob departed, the rarely relenting sadness returned in force. I had to face it. This was depression. Although I had always said it could not happen to a serious Christian—and I considered myself that—I was depressed. The evidence was simply undeniable.

This conclusion brought a shaky relief somehow. At the same time it raised questions: How could this have happened? Had I been disobeying God? Was there sin in my life? Was this my fault?

Late afternoon found Carey and me comparing notes of our diary findings. I did not mention my new and amazing conclusion about being depressed. It was only my conclusion, after all. I had not yet had time to consider the questions now forming in my mind. But I could already tell they were leading me to challenge a strongly held opinion. Everything I had read about depression said that the person who recognized those symptoms in himself should consult a doctor. And any doctor who diagnosed depression in me would likely treat it as an illness. I had always said that depression was not physiological in basis, but spiritual. Yet in my tired and battered mind, I could not identify any spiritual cause for this.

No, I would delay my talk with Carey. After all, a doctor had confirmed nothing yet.

But still I kept casting about.

How will Carey react, I asked myself, *when I tell him I may be depressed? What if there is some loss of our mutual and delightful understanding of each other? I don't think he could ever experience the depth of sadness I now feel. Will it cause a wedge in our oneness?*

I did not welcome the thought.

Carey and I prayed together about the new year of 1996 and laid it in God's hands. And silently, not knowing exactly what to ask, I entreated the Lord for help.

Snow fell that evening in Grand Prairie, and Carey stoked the fire often. We pulled our chairs close to it and to each other, and read, and talked. More questions arose in my mind. I kept them to myself.

If this was depression, would my doctor send me to a psychiatrist? Perish the thought! Would I be prescribed medication? I could not handle that. Would I need some special counsel? I was skeptical of many of the claims of psychiatry.

Now and then Carey and I glanced out the window into the darkness. It was still snowing. Would it stay? Probably not in Texas.

As I had grown up in Hastings in the county of Sussex, on the southeast coast of England, a white world would sometimes greet me in the morning when I looked out my bedroom window. That world seemed eons away. Since then I had lived and worked as a mission volunteer in Kenya, East Africa. I had spent seven years in the Netherlands with Dutch missionary Brother Andrew, helping with his work on behalf of the suffering Church in Communist countries. And I had spent the last seven years of her life as companion to Corrie ten Boom, a Dutch missionary who had committed her life to telling of the love of God as she experienced it in a Nazi concentration camp.

I had been away from England for thirty years. I had become a Christian leader myself. If depression were professionally diagnosed, should I admit it at my place of work and to my friends and family? If so, what would those people think who looked up to me as a strong Christian? I did not want to appear weak, and a diagnosis of depression, after all, would surely indicate serious weakness! I wanted to appear strong and normal, not weak and crazy.

Most important of all, what about the Gospel? Was I not disappointing the Lord Jesus Christ? Where was the joyful Christian I had once been? What was happening to me?

Into the Unknown

"Again, I tell you that if two of you on earth agree about anything you ask for, it will be done for you by my Father in heaven."

Matthew 18:19

Nearly three weeks passed before I summoned enough courage to visit our family doctor in the adjacent city of Arlington. He listened carefully as I described my symptoms and confirmed that I was suffering from clinical depression (*clinical* means an illness requiring medical treatment). Then, in a most hope-giving way, he explained the treatment he thought would be best for me. I remember leaving his office with a sense of relief that I had been listened to—and also with a sense of amazement at the number of patients he told me were under his care for the same ailment.

"What did the doctor say?" asked Carey as soon as we were together in our blue and white home after work that evening in late January.

Because making tea is always the first thing I do on arriving home, even before preparing dinner, we stood in the kitchen while I waited for the kettle to boil.

"He confirmed what I'd begun to suspect," I replied. "It is clinical depression."

Still standing, his burgundy briefcase set down beside him, Carey listened with his usual careful kindness as I explained how my symptoms tallied with those of many other patients under the doctor's care, and as I described his advice.

I was aware that a mysterious and (to me) new field of developing knowledge on depression was lying before me waiting to be trodden and then explored. Not yet knowing how to step into that rather forbidding field, I could not find fluent expression of my thoughts as I talked to my husband that evening. But I tried to communicate to him the fact that I could now see that my type of debilitating depression had to be an illness. For what reason a person became debilitatingly (clinically) depressed, I did not know. But I could feel and see that I was ill, and that I needed treatment.

Soon we were sitting at the kitchen table, our cups of tea in front of us. For some time I poured out to Carey how on New Year's Day I had faced the possibility of clinical depression.

"It was almost as if I were addressing another person," I told him, trying to describe the conversation between the old Pam and the new, sad one. "I had to admit that the way I was feeling was not the normal me and that there had to be a reason why."

"I didn't realize how bad you've been feeling," Carey said. "And I'm so sorry about that. I wish I'd seen it."

"But clinical depression cannot be seen," I replied. "If I had a broken leg, you could see it. But this illness is so mysterious and so internal."

Although it was a relief to describe depression for the first time as an illness, inside I knew that this was not a complete description. What had led to the illness, for example?

Carey got up, leaned over, took me in his arms and hugged me, as I mumbled into his shoulder, "I have even been wondering if a diagnosis of clinical depression will affect our relationship."

"How could it do that," he replied, "since we are in this together?"

We talked for a long time. How should we proceed? Together we were on a new journey into the unknown, involving continuing chemotherapy for Carey and treatment for depression for me. We kept talking while we prepared supper together, and after eating we prayed—an activity we have engaged in almost every day since the beginning of our marriage.

I soon learned that my fears regarding the effect this diagnosis would have on our marriage were groundless—a by-product of my own anxiety and misapprehensions. Rather than force a wedge between us, my diagnosis drew us together as we sought better understanding of clinical depression. In fact, most of the fears I had anticipated concerning what Carey and others in the Christian community might think about my being clinically depressed have turned out to be phantoms.

And my fear of losing Carey quickly to the unknown malignancy turned out to be a ghost as well. At the time of this writing, nearly five years after his diagnosis, Carey is healthy, and proves it by such feats as keeping up his regular running through hundred-degree Texas summer heat.

Though my fears proved needless, in the sense that I was not to lose Carey quickly, they were not valueless. Because life traumas can cause emotional devastation and actually affect brain chemistry, it is likely that my fears, as well as the complication of other developments in my life at that time (I will talk about some of these in chapter 8), helped propel me to a point of desperation. Healing could begin only at the point that the second Pam began to admit her need of help.

Perhaps you, too, need help. Perhaps you, like the first Pam, have always believed that depression has a solely spiritual basis. Perhaps you are afraid to admit you might need to see a doctor regarding depression because it would only confirm that you have failed to lead a victorious Christian life. If so, be encouraged. In the chapters that follow you will see how the second Pam, the one who began to realize she was suffering from an illness, found help and healing.

At the same time, I do not believe depression can be "justified" only if it is described as an illness requiring medical treatment. There is much more to it than that, more than our scientists and theologians yet know.

I want to share with you some of the lessons I learned and am still learning while going through and coming out of common clinical depression. We will explore several elements of this disease—for faulty biochemistry is not the only trigger of depression. A lack of spiritual vigilance can also allow depression to come into a person's life; so can life circumstances and emotional chain reactions, as in my case. And while professional help is very important, there are some instances in which an individual also needs to turn to inner resolve, with the Lord's help, and bravely face personal areas that need to change in order to be successful in the fight against depression.

I sincerely wish not to throw any generalized answers over a very serious and often baffling illness, or to suggest that everybody shares the particular symptoms that accompanied my own case.

As my recovery began, I resumed speaking appointments at churches and conferences. When appropriate, I began to refer to my depression in my talks. And in nearly every meeting, the response has been the same: tears of relief and gratitude when people learn they can put a name to the affliction they have suffered silently. And, yes, occasionally the response is one of shock and disapproval: "But how can it happen to a *Christian*?" I hope this book will help answer that question.

In fact, I would like this book to do two things: first, to bring comfort and help to anyone who is depressed; and second, to help Christians who have never been depressed to recognize the Lord Jesus Christ in hurting individuals and find ways to better love and care for them.

Let's step back and look at a bigger part of the picture. If the two main purposes of this book are reached in the lives of even a few of us, they could have the larger effect of helping many depressed Christians remove the masks they wear to shield themselves from hurt caused by rejection in the Church. And if we step back even further, we might see, in faith, an even grander part of the picture—that you and I can have an important part in showing the world that Christians really do love each other.

Defining Depression

The word *depression,* as we will see in a few examples in this chapter, can refer to anything from a passing mood to a major illness. Since most Christians do not hold degrees in psychiatry or psychology, the subject can seem too forbidding to investigate. Some of us reckon that since even psychiatrists and psychologists admit that ever-deepening oceans of knowledge concerning their medical specialties leave them with new mysteries to fathom, it would not be of much use for us to dabble in the shallows.

Other Christians, though fewer in number, dismiss depression altogether and regard psychiatry and psychology with suspicion. I used to be one of these. In my younger years I frequently declared, "Psychiatry is bunk!" Up until the time of my own diagnosis, I tried to ignore growing evidence that depression is a disease that afflicts even believers. I preferred to stay safely among the ranks of those serious and sincere Christians who hold that depression has no medical basis. This unsympathetic attitude takes the stance that depression is always a result of blatant or unconscious sin that has brought separation from God and, therefore, misery. A Christian should always be joyful.

I decided years ago that it was best to avoid the subject of depression because it challenged the validity and stability of my faith. After all, if depression and its negative, joyless symptoms were of medical origin, then a strong assertion of faith in the Lord Jesus Christ was not enough to maintain healthy living. It was easier for me to stand behind a deeply rooted tradition than to accept the challenge of investigating the mystery of mental illness. I stood behind that tradition for a long time, in spite of decades of travel and a lot of hard work in Christian ministry. Unfortunately my misconceptions left me ill-equipped to help those I met in my travels who were suffering from depression.

Since Jesus Christ became Lord of my life when I was 21 years old, I have loved Him deeply. On a March day in 1965, I surrendered to Him what I had regarded as my right to my own way. Ever since that surrender, the fact of the coming Judgment Seat of Christ held no fear for me. The Son of Man will one day sit on his throne in heavenly glory with all the nations in front of Him. He will separate the nations from one another as a Middle Eastern shepherd would separate sheep from goats, the sheep on the right and the goats on the left.

> "Then the King will say to those on his right, 'Come, you who are blessed by my Father; take your inheritance, the kingdom prepared for you since the creation of the world. For I was hungry and you gave me something to eat, I was thirsty and you gave me something to drink, I was a stranger and you invited me in, I needed clothes and you clothed me, I was sick and you looked after me, I was in prison and you came to visit me.'
>
> "Then the righteous will answer him, 'Lord, when did we see you hungry and feed you, or thirsty and give you something to drink? When did we see you a stranger and invite you in, or needing clothes and clothe you? When did we see you sick or in prison and go to visit you?'
>
> "The King will reply, 'I tell you the truth, whatever you did for one of the least of these brothers of mine, you did for me.'"
>
> Matthew 25:34–40

Although I knew I could never do enough, it delighted me to think that compassion and kindness shown in actual deeds to the hungry, thirsty, the stranger, the poor, the ill and the prisoner were received by the Lord Jesus as really done for Him. The years had held many opportunities to give practical help to others, including long-term nursing of the sick. But it took my own eventual diagnosis of depression to show me that for years I had failed to minister to the Lord Jesus Christ in dozens of depressed people around me.

Suppose I had not received a diagnosis of the disease. Could the Lord Jesus still have used me to display His compassion and love to the depressed? Of course He could! The Lord can do anything. But for years I felt not only unsympathetic but also judgmental. I am gaining understanding rather late but, thank God, it is not too late! It is never too late for anybody to seek understanding.

In my search for more understanding, I have read books, articles and Internet sources about depression. For example, Robert E. Emery and Thomas F. Oltmanns in their book *Essentials of Abnormal Psychology* (Prentice-Hall, 2000) gave me the following helpful information:

> Depression can refer either to a mood or to a clinical syndrome—a combination of emotional, cognitive, and behavioral symptoms. The feelings associated with a *depressed mood* often include disappointment and despair. Although sadness is a universal experience, profound depression is not. People who are in a severely depressed mood describe the feeling as overwhelming, suffocating or numbing. In the syndrome of depression, which is also called *clinical depression*, a depressed mood is accompanied by several other symptoms, such as fatigue, loss of energy, difficulty in sleeping, and changes in appetite. Clinical depression also involves a variety of changes in thinking and overt behavior. The person may experience cognitive symptoms, such as extreme guilt, feelings of worthlessness, concentration problems, and

thoughts of suicide. Behavioral symptoms may range from constant pacing and fidgeting to extreme inactivity.

With the above description in mind, I will use the term *depression* throughout the rest of this book to refer to the clinical syndrome (a group of signs or symptoms that occur together and characterize a particular abnormality) rather than to the mood.

Common Forms of Depression

Although depression occurs in many forms, let's investigate the three most common.

We all know the feelings of despondency and pessimism that can accompany life's disappointments, but that are usually temporary. These feelings are often termed *depression* in everyday, casual, nonmedical conversation, but they are not true depression. We see an example of this kind of sadness in Amy, a nineteen-year-old student at Dallas Baptist University. (Her name and many others in this book have been changed to protect privacy.) Amy came to work at my office as usual one afternoon last summer, but my first glance at her normally bright face told me that a calamity had taken place in her life.

"What's happened, Amy?"

"I've just learned that I've lost my scholarship for next year," she replied, breaking down in tears. She went on to explain that her grade point average was too low to maintain her scholarship.

So upset was she that I suggested she curtail her work activities for the afternoon.

The usually sunny Amy was sad for several days, but it was not long before her smile and optimism returned. She began to see that the loss was not as devastating as it had first seemed. The university's administration rallied around her; so did her family and friends. She continued to study her Bible and pray, as was her daily habit. Several short-term and long-term possible solutions gave new hope. She would be able to stay at the university after all.

In about a week's time, Amy's emotional responses were normal and healthy. She needed no more time off, and the future welcomed and challenged her as it always had. She was not ill. Hers was a temporary and normal (nonclinical) depression—the result of a loss.

All of us can identify with what Amy experienced. And many of us can identify with a second, more complicated kind of depression. We know the emotional anguish that can accompany major loss such as divorce, the death of a loved one or being let go from a job. These losses involve deeper and longer sadness than Amy's, but such sadness is still natural. Most people recover in lengths of time proportionate to the depth of the loss and, since we are all different, to our own ways of dealing with loss.

An example is Joe, a friend of ours whose wife divorced him a couple of years ago. Joe was devastated. He lost weight, seemed to spend every waking hour working and, for a while, retreated from contact with other co-workers. Joe had suffered a major loss and was depressed. It would have been abnormal for him not to be depressed. But it took him longer to recover than it did Amy. A serious Christian, he prayed and studied his Bible, as he had always done, and received encouragement and counsel from Christian friends. Gradually he recovered emotional balance. Joe was never so seriously disabled by his grief and resulting depression that his life and work were affected. And although his loss was enormous, Joe recovered.

The third kind, clinical depression, is a serious illness that requires treatment. It is much more complicated in nature than Joe's kind of depression and is usually the result of a number of factors, as well as of major loss. This is the kind that afflicted me. I would describe this as the type of depression in which the sufferer experiences symptoms that affect nearly every aspect of living. He does not feel like himself; she cannot function normally. The main symptoms are:

- A sad, anxious or empty mood that lasts for two weeks or more
- Loss of interest or pleasure in most activities that before were enjoyable
- Feelings of hopelessness, worthlessness, guilt and helplessness
- Significant changes in weight or appetite
- Changes in sleep habits (such as insomnia or over-sleeping)
- Fatigue, loss of energy; feeling "slowed down"
- Agitation, restlessness, irritability
- Difficulty concentrating, making decisions
- Frequent thoughts of death or suicide, or suicide attempts

I came to know Helena some twenty years ago when I lived in Orange County, California. She was a young woman who, with her husband, had come from South Africa to study at a Bible college. Helena was outgoing, vivacious and highly motivated. Then a serious car accident ended her studies. Shortly after her partial recovery from her injuries, she disappeared. Mystified by this for several weeks, I learned that Helena had gone to stay with Christian friends in another part of the state. It was many months before I saw her again, but one day she reappeared and came to visit me.

At the time I could not understand why she had avoided her friends or spent those months in isolation, but looking back I realize that she had been overcome by major clinical depression. Helena had been very ill. I learned that she had experienced nearly all the symptoms listed above and was severely disabled. She had needed time and treatment to recover. Since this took place twenty years ago, when mental illness held a much higher stigma, she received little understanding and support from fellow Christians. But Helena did recover. She and her husband returned to their native country, were given the children she had always longed for and began full-time ministry at a Christian youth camp.

During her time of depression, she told me, Helena read her Bible and prayed as faithfully as ever. She did all she knew to pull herself out of a depression during which she could hardly get up in the mornings. At some point her emotional state had crossed the frightening line from "normal" to "abnormal."

It was like that with my case of depression, too. Why were Helena and I not like Joe? He had suffered loss through divorce but was able to live a fairly normal life and continue with his daily work. I had suffered loss by the diagnosis of an often-fatal type of malignancy in my husband but, unlike Joe, I became too ill to function normally.

As we proceed together through these pages, we will see that every case of depression is different. It cannot usually be traced to one particular cause. We can never make sweeping generalizations as we seek, in the spirit of Christ, to understand and help the depressed.

The events of life, although not the whole cause, can lead to clinical depression. Some people receive crushing blows and do well. It is not the blow, but what the blow means to that particular person, with her previous life experiences and particular emotional makeup, that can lead to clinical depression. What constitutes a crushing blow to one person may not make much of an emotional impression on another. God knows what He needs to do in each of our lives to make us more like the Lord Jesus. Are we relying on our own strength? If so God will point that out, because He loves us.

The stories of student Amy (who found herself with normal, short-term sadness, not depression in the medical sense), friend Joe (who had longer-term normal depression) and Helena (whose depression caused clinical depression in which she became too ill to function normally) are general examples.

The question could arise: If clinical depression is medical, then do emotional events initiate its onset or only exacerbate it? Would Helena have become clinically depressed if she had not had the accident? I do not know, and neither, I respectfully submit, does anybody else except her Maker. As in the case of most of us, Helena had undoubtedly experienced other losses. Loss often leads to depression. Helena's accident may have caused temporary brain damage or emotional trauma, which combined with previous losses were too hard for her to bear. Helena is unique, different from anybody else the Lord has ever made. Who can say at what point her depth of loss and her particular way of dealing with that loss crossed the frightening line between "normal" and "abnormal" depression?

Since so many people, including Christians, are affected by clinical depression, it is imperative that all of us, depressed and non-depressed Christians alike, gain deeper understanding and knowledge.

Why Is This Illness Called Depression?

As we have said, depression has many causes and cannot be generalized. Nor is it always easy to recognize in those around us, even those close to us. Depression also has many more forms than the three I have just described. It would be helpful if the various manifestations of the disease had names, but this naming has not taken place. I suppose this is because of its complexity. Thus we are faced with a variety of clinical manifestations of depression (and other mental health disorders of which depression is part), and only one name for it.

William Styron, in his excellent book *Darkness Visible: A Memoir of Madness* (Random House, 1990), describes it this way:

> When I was first aware that I had been laid low by the disease, I felt a need, among other things, to register a strong protest against the word "depression." Depression, most people know, used to be termed "melancholia," a word which appears in English as early as the year 1303 and crops up more than once in Chaucer, who in his usage seemed to be

aware of its pathological nuances. "Melancholia" would still appear to be a far more apt and evocative word for the blacker forms of the disorder. . . .

As one who has suffered from the malady in extremis yet returned to tell the tale, I would lobby for a truly arresting designation. "Brainstorm," for instance, has unfortunately been preempted to describe, somewhat jocularly, intellectual inspiration. But something along these lines is needed. Told that someone's mood disorder has evolved into a storm—a veritable howling tempest in the brain, which is indeed what a clinical depression resembles like nothing else—even the uninformed layman might display sympathy rather than the standard reaction that "depression" evokes, something akin to "So what?" or "You'll pull out of it" or "We all have bad days." The phrase "nervous breakdown" seems to be on its way out, certainly deservedly so, owing to its insinuation of a vague spinelessness, but we still seem destined to be saddled with "depression" until a better, sturdier name is created.

In the coming pages I want to mainly address this common emotional illness that is called, for lack of a more descriptive noun, clinical depression. (Let's remind ourselves again that *clinical* means the depression requires medical attention.) Common clinical depression is a malady by which we are all surrounded. Although you may not be aware of it, you know several people who have this malady, and there are millions more sufferers throughout the world. If you and I do not seek understanding and pray to be shown how to act like the Lord Jesus in applying this understanding, we will fail to minister to Him in countless people who suffer from common clinical depression.

Whether you are depressed yourself, or you are a well Christian wanting to help the depressed, or you are a well Christian not yet ready to identify with the depressed, will you accompany me in seeking better understanding?

Who Is Affected by Depression?

3

How long must I wrestle with my thoughts and every day have sorrow in my heart?

Psalm 13:2

Depression can happen to anybody. Those who say, as I once did, "It could never happen to me," are just as likely to succumb to it as anybody else. Depression can occur, moreover, at any age.

Since statistical studies vary in their criteria for diagnosis, and since many people never seek treatment and remain undiagnosed, it is difficult to obtain accurate information about how common the disease is. In 1985 it was estimated that nine million people in the United States were victims of depression. In 1999 depression was thought to afflict nearly eighteen million Americans, of whom only six million received treatment. Some mental health professionals predict that by the year 2020, depression will be second only to heart disease as the world's most disabling illness. It has been estimated that the lifetime prevalence for depression is between seventeen and twenty percent, meaning that between seventeen and twenty percent of the population can expect to become depressed at some point in their lifetimes. Some believe the percentage is much higher. In any case it is clearly rising.

These figures refer to Americans in general without reference to religious beliefs. There is no conclusive evidence of any relationship between religion and depressive symptoms. It is likely, however, that the stigma and shame of depression are higher in Christian circles, making it probable that churches hold many depressed Christians who choose not to admit it. Statistics suggest that women are more susceptible to the disease than men, but the incidence in men is probably higher than reported, since men are less willing to admit the possibility of depression and therefore do not seek help.

Most suicides are the result of depression. There is a fifteen percent risk of a depressed person seeking to end her or his life. Two groups in particular have undergone an alarming rise in suicide attempts and successes: young people and the elderly.

Depression and Suicide in Children and Young People

More and more teenagers seem to be turning to suicide as a desperate solution to seemingly insoluble problems. Suicide is the sixth leading cause of death for youngsters ages 5 to 14, and the third leading cause of death for young people ages 15 to 24. According to Dr. Alan Berman, former president of the American Association of Suicidology, the youngest reported case of suicide is a four-year-old.

Depression in Children

Ashley, age seven, receives counseling because of very stressful circumstances in her family. She told her counselor that she sometimes got so sad that she wanted to ride her bicycle out of her front gate and into the traffic on the wide street beside her home. She was serious about this desire, telling her counselor she was so sad at times that she really wanted a car to run over her so she could die.

When the counselor reported this to Ashley's parents, they could not believe it and were very upset. Because of their daughter's high risk for suicide, in light of her stress level and definite plan, the therapist recommended that Ashley be admitted to the hospital. Her father refused to allow this. He could see that Ashley was troubled, but maintained that he would certainly know if his daughter was serious in wanting to die.

Emily, thirteen years old, attended a Christian summer camp with her parents, elder sister and younger brother, a yearly tradition for this close and loving family. Although nobody in the family knew it at the time, Emily had been having what her mother later described to me as "dreadful thoughts." A sincere Christian, Emily went to the camp bookstore one day and purchased *Peace with God* by Billy Graham. That night, taking care not to wake the others, Emily went quietly to the bathroom of their cabin, turned on a small flashlight and began to read. Hoping to find the peace for which she desperately longed, she searched and searched in the pages of the book. What was wrong? Why could she not find peace with God?

Emily recalled this incident years later when as a young adult she succumbed to major depression. As she explained to her mother, she had sincerely received Christ as her Savior when she was a child, but had never known the inner peace she sought so desperately. Emily is receiving medical treatment now and is responding.

Emily's sharing of her lonely childhood secret reminded me of my own painful early years. In Hastings, Sussex, on the southeast coast of England, I was the eldest of three children. Ours was a stable and loving home. When I was about five I accepted Jesus Christ as my Savior. Although it was not until I was 21 that I began to follow Him closely, His presence was always real to me. I talked to Him often, especially about some things I did not understand. I seemed to be different from my happier and more confident younger brother and sister and, as far as I knew, from the other boys and girls at West St. Leonards Infants, Primary and Junior Schools as well.

Why, for instance, was I so terrified of answering questions put to the class by our teachers? The idea of giving a wrong answer was so mortifying that I dared not take the risk. I did not detect this fear in my brother or sister. And why did I keep up certain behaviors that I felt compelled to do but that I knew were not normal?

This, for instance. The bedroom that my sister, Sylvia, and I shared opened to the same landing as the room our brother, Digger, slept in. In addition there was a common door between the two rooms. This made for some happy children's tag and hide-and-seek games when the door was open during the day. At night, however, the inner door was a problem for me. When our parents said goodnight to us, they closed the door between the two bedrooms and turned out the lights. Soon after they left I would slip out of bed to test the door. Was it really shut? I could not convince myself that it was. Sometimes I shut it three times, sometimes five sets of three times, very quietly, trying not to disturb my brother and sister. I knew this action was not necessary. The door was shut. I could see that it was shut. But I could not convince myself that it really was.

This was abnormal and it made me miserable. Why was I compelled to do it? And to check ten times that the burners on the stove were turned off? Or to cross back and forth over a particular mark on the pavement twelve times, as if life could not move forward unless I did?

Sometimes I prayed, *Lord Jesus, please help me not to do these strange things.* And desperately, now and then: *I promise You I will not do these strange things.*

As time went by and I entered my teen years, the intensity of the compulsions lessened, but I was never quite free of them. Perhaps it was because of this peculiar handicap, through which I recognized that my nervous system was less hardy than that of other children, that I determined to be and to appear as strong as possible. I could not talk about this oddity to anybody except my mother, and since I did not know how to describe it, I am not sure she understood. But she listened with love to her eldest child, telling me that as time went on I would "grow out of it." This proved true to a degree.

I should mention that I was a gloomy, complaining child. The word *miserable* is the description my parents and brother and sister found most apt when recalling my childhood! I must add that all four were patient with me, although they could not understand why I did not share the sunny dispositions of Sylvia and Digger. I could not blame them; I could not understand it either.

I feel sure now that I was a depressed child who also suffered from obsessive-compulsive tendencies. As far as I know, information about obsessive-compulsive disorder (OCD) was not available to the average family in the 1940s and '50s when I was a child. It was not until I received medical treatment for depression (which I will describe in chapter 8) that I was able to see how to break the cycle of OCD. How thankful we can be that many children no longer need to suffer in the way that I and many others did! This tendency or disorder can be recognized and treated, often successfully.

I addressed a group of women leaders gathered at a church in McKinney, Texas, a few years back. Many of them spoke to me afterward, including a schoolteacher who talked quickly and urgently. "Through what you told us of the symptoms of depression," she said, "I can see that one of the children in my class may be depressed. How can I get him the help he needs?"

I think about that little boy sometimes and wonder how he is doing. I thank God for his sensitive teacher who recognized that something was wrong! Was she or the school nurse able to persuade his parents to seek help? May there be many more of us who keep a close lookout for depression in children. Teachers have more than enough to do already; it takes watchfulness by all of us who touch children's lives to see that the particularly needy ones receive help.

The behavior of depressed children and teenagers may differ from the behavior of depressed adults. Here is a list of signs of depression in children, compiled by the American Academy of Child and Adolescent Psychiatry in "Facts for Families: The Depressed Child":

- Frequent sadness, tearfulness, crying
- Hopelessness
- Decreased interest in activities
- Persistent boredom, low energy
- Social isolation
- Poor communication
- Low self-esteem; guilt
- Extreme sensitivity or reaction to failure
- Increased irritability, anger or hostility
- Difficulty with relationships
- Frequent complaints of physical illness such as headaches or stomachaches
- Frequent absences from school or poor performance in school
- Poor concentration
- Major changes in eating and/or sleeping patterns
- Talk of or efforts to run away from home
- Thoughts or expressions of suicide or self-destructive behavior

If you are in any doubt about a child's mental health, seek a way for him or her to receive a checkup. If you know that a youngster is contemplating suicide, alert the authorities. As in the case of young Ashley, who wanted to ride her bike into traffic, parents often refuse to believe such deliberations could even be possible. Ask the Lord to dispel any denial you may have, if necessary. We must humble ourselves, admit the possibility, pray and take action if we have any suspicion that a child may be clinically depressed.

Depression in Teenagers and Young Adults

Jonathan is a student at Dallas Baptist University. Because his parents knew about my experience with clinical depression, they confided to me that Jonathan was suffering from the same ailment and was receiving treatment. I asked them to tell their son that if he ever felt like talking to me, I was available. One day during the second week of a new school year, he came to my office.

A handsome, muscular young man, Jonathan was open about his feelings. He said he felt completely overwhelmed and exhausted. He was unable to eat properly and never sensed that he measured up. He described his fear of dating: "The girls see this good-looking guy, but inside I cannot cope at all."

Jonathan was a committed Christian. He studied and believed the Bible. But in the depths of his depression, it was not possible for him to receive any solace that I tried to bring through Scripture.

"I know and believe what you are saying," he said, weeping. "But it doesn't help me feel better." Then he added with the deep sighing that often accompanies major depression, "It would seem from the Bible that Christians should not feel like this."

Jonathan was not looking for an answer from me that day. But his statement needs a response in the hearts and minds of all of us who will face God's Judgment Seat one day and will hear the Lord's words, "I was sick and you. . . ." How often do we agree, silently or otherwise, with the notion that the depressed person should just "get over it" or "pull himself together"? How often do we give pat answers to the hurting, telling them that the Bible has the solution to their problems but never taking the time to be the understanding friend they need or to look after the sufferer as looking after the Lord?

Granted, talks with young people like Jonathan are not easy for anybody at first, whether a professional in the mental health field or an ordinary Christian like you and me. But we should not be afraid of such conversations. The more we practice, the less difficult they become. The depressed have a deep need for non-judgmental communication. Jonathan did not want or need from me a long or complicated answer to his statement. And he certainly did not need me to say something like, "Just keep trusting the Lord."

So despairing was Jonathan that day that I asked him respectfully if he was contemplating suicide. From his reply I believed he was not, but I knew I had to be as sure as possible before he left my office. As the university's prayer ministry leader, I had to walk the fine line between confidentiality and reporting potentially self-destructive behavior. If he had given any indication that he was planning suicide, I would have been under obligation to report the matter to mental health professionals.

After more conversation, Jonathan said, "I came for prayer. Will you pray for me?"

I did and, with his permission, asked others to pray without giving them his name, as he requested. Jonathan did not want to share his depression with other students. He did not want to be treated differently, he told me. But before he left, to my relief, he gave me permission to share his need with a male student his own age whom I knew could be trusted to keep Jonathan's secret. That student lived in the dorm, as did Jonathan, and would be available should Jonathan have a special need at any time.

Jonathan still struggles with depression, but he has a supportive family who is knowledgeable about his illness. He attends a Christian university where students reach out to each other in greater measure than probably takes place on a secular campus. And Jonathan is prayed for.

What about the large numbers of depressed teens and young people in society at large who do not have the kind of support Jonathan has? Here is a list of behaviors, also compiled by the American Academy of Child and Adolescent Psychiatry, that could indicate severe depression in young people. If anybody comes to mind as you read the following indicators, even if he or she is not your own child, please discuss that person with his or her family member, an adult trusted friend or even a young trusted friend. Sometimes it is harder for the people nearest the depressed young person to recognize serious warning signs of suicidal depression than it is for somebody like you or me, who can view the person involved more objectively.

- An abrupt change in personality, dress, style, interests, friends
- Withdrawal or isolation, especially if the young person has always been gregarious and outgoing
- Alcohol or drug use
- Signs of self-mutilation
- Violent behavior—punching holes into walls, getting into fights, self-destructive violence
- A consistent pattern of running away from home
- Significant change in sleeping patterns (suddenly sleeps all the time or does not sleep at all)
- Neglect of personal appearance (most adolescents want to look their best, even if their idea of looking good is at odds with yours or mine)
- Lingering lethargy, a dropoff in schoolwork

- Loss of interest in recreational activities
- Lack of interest in praise or rewards
- Weepiness, abrupt or constant crying
- Expressions of low self-esteem, feelings of worthlessness ("I'm no good")
- References to the fact that she will not be around much longer to be a burden to everyone
- Indications that he is overwhelmed ("What difference does it make?" or "Life makes no sense")
- Actions that reflect sudden interest in giving important or favorite possessions away, putting his affairs in order, making amends, saying good-bye
- Sudden and unaccountable cheerfulness, sense of relief or resoluteness after an extended period of depression

Teenage and young adult suicide rates are rising. In addition to praying for the parents of the young people you know, ask God that your local high school teachers and coaches, employers, fellow students, church leaders and others may be given insight and seek help for the deeply troubled young people who really need it.

Depression in Senior Adults

In 1900 the average life span for a man was 46 years, and for a woman, 48 years. A century later the figures have grown to 73 and 80 respectively. While today's senior citizens—those who are 65 and older—represent about thirteen percent of the population, they commit some twenty percent of all suicides. White males over the age of 85 take their own lives at a rate almost six times the national average.

Not long ago Jim Roland paid an unexpected visit to my office. In his seventies, he is a leader in his local church ministry to seniors. Before the death of his wife, Roberta, a few years back, the couple had attended several campus events. Glad to see him, I fixed us cups of coffee as Jim began to tell me about being restored to health after suffering serious depression.

After Roberta's death, Jim had experienced loss of appetite, sleeplessness and general sadness. Because he had known milder versions of these symptoms all his life, he said, he did not pay too much attention to them. Something happened, however, that sounded a strong warning bell.

Before her death Jim and Roberta had planned a cruise to Scandinavia. Afterward, since the vacation was already paid for, Jim decided to go alone. One evening after a stroll on the deck, he leaned against the ship's outer railing. He gazed out to sea, then came to focus on the dark water below him. All at once the waves seemed to beckon him; he found it an attractive idea to jump in. Somehow he was able to push back from the rail and return to his cabin.

So shaken was Jim by that frightening experience that when he returned home, he heeded the urgings of a retired nurse in his church's senior adult fellowship to see his doctor. He was diagnosed with clinical depression and put on medication.

As Jim and I sat in my office with our cups of coffee that morning, I marveled at his willingness to admit to having depression. Many elderly consider it a serious sign of weakness and do not want to discuss it. But Jim was so delighted with his newfound health that he wanted to tell me about it. The sense of sadness and unworthiness he had felt, and his tendency to withdraw from others—all of which he had suffered from childhood—had left him since he had begun the medication.

Curious, I asked Jim if there had been any events in his childhood that had made him sad.

"My father did not show me much love and encouragement," he replied. "He often told me I would never amount to anything."

If I were a mental health professional and could talk at length with Jim, I would probably have a better idea about the effects on Jim's life of his father's unkindness. But I cannot help wondering: Did the father's belittling of his son bring on Jim's sense of unworthiness as an adult? Or was Jim born with a predisposition to depression through, perhaps, brain damage at birth or a genetic tendency? Genetic abnormalities can affect neurotransmitters that send nerve impulses across synapses between brain cells. What if the pathways in Jim's brain could not relay efficient signals from one brain cell to the next for consistently healthy emotional responses? Was his father, seeing in Jim a timid and tentative child, reacting to evidence of such a disorder? In other words, did the father's actions bring on the depression, or was a congenital depression simply made worse by an insensitive father?

Perhaps both are true. In any case, I celebrate with Jim Roland the fact that the later years of his life are being spent with a new confidence in who he is in Christ and without a heavy spirit.

Many seniors, however, have sad conclusions to their stories. As I said earlier, depression leads to suicide in the senior adult age bracket more often than in any other segment of the population. Suicide attempts are not only more frequent but better thought through and more likely to end in death. Someone aged 65 or older takes his or her life every ninety minutes, accounting for sixteen deaths each day.

Losses and grief are compounded for the elderly. Many have lost their spouses and suffer declining health. Through lessening strength, they are no longer able to take part in activities they once enjoyed, and as years proceed they lose more of their siblings and friends. Marie, an 86-year-old friend of mine, is deeply mourning the loss of her friend Thelma, whom she had known all her life. Her grief is just as great as that of my young friend Tammy, who recently experienced the sudden death of her friend Katy, whom she had known since kindergarten. Even though the death of an elderly person is expected it is no less painful to her friends.

It is important to watch for signs of depression in elderly relatives and friends. Take note of listlessness, hopelessness and changes in sleep or appetite that are indicated in clinical depression, and also of the following:

- Cutting back on social interaction, self-care and grooming
- Breaking medical regimens (for example, going off diets or prescriptions)
- Putting affairs in order, giving things away, making changes in wills
- Stockpiling medication or obtaining other potentially lethal paraphernalia

Other clues are preoccupation with death or lack of concern about personal safety. Good-byes such as "This is the last time that you'll see me" or "I won't be needing any more appointments" should signal alarm.

Who Else Is Affected by Depression?

Common clinical depression is not only the most common form of depression, but it is also associated with many major brain disorders. Those suffering from bipolar disorder and schizophrenia, for example, also know the desolation of major clinical depression. I mention these two disorders because Carey and I have good friends who suffer from them, but there are many other mental illnesses of which depression is part.

Vivian, who lives in California, is high on the list of people I most admire. I have known her for nearly thirty years. Her brain disorder, which has been hard to diagnose, is at this time considered to be "traumatic brain injury and associated major recurrent depression."

As I discussed the subject of this book with her, she helped me see how complex clinical depression is. For example, she is one of many sufferers of major depression whose illness manifests psychotic features. A layman's definition of *psychosis* is "severe mental derangement involving the whole personality." Vivian has not been diagnosed with psychosis, but because of the psychotic-like symptoms that accompany her major depression, she has to take antipsychotic medicine.

What a long way we have to go in reaching out with the love of the Lord Jesus to those with major brain disorders!

But let's press on in our journey of discovery about common clinical depression—the illness you and I are most likely to encounter in our daily lives.

Is Depression My Fault?

There is now no condemnation for those who are in Christ Jesus.

Romans 8:1

Peggy e-mailed me from Oklahoma City after I spoke to the women in her church not long after the bombing at the Alfred P. Murrah Federal Building in 1995:

> I have been on medication for depression for several years. I have tried to stop taking it but do not do well if I do. I feel such a failure, so guilty. Why is the Lord not enough? But even as I write those words I must say that I know enough about the disease to realize that this is the disease talking.

Sara, one of my co-workers, e-mailed me, too:

> I am praying for your book about Christians and depression. I am going

through a terrible time of depression at the moment and feel so guilty and ashamed.

Guilt is feeling bad about what we do. Shame is feeling bad about who we are. Why did these two Christian women feel guilty and ashamed? If they had deliberately sinned against God, guilt and shame would be a natural consequence, since the Holy Spirit's work is to show us our sin. But had they sinned against God in a deliberate way? They could not point to any sin, and deliberate sin was not evident to their friends. Were they really guilty? If not, the emotion they were feeling was surely false guilt. And since they were suffering already with clinical depression, a miserable situation was being made worse by their self-accusation of wrongdoing.

Perhaps the shame and guilt were internal reactions to comments from those who believe that committed Christians should never be depressed. Or perhaps the shame was generated from an emotionally warped perception of how other Christians might perceive them, even if there was no reason to expect condemnation.

When the depressed Christian's brain circles endlessly through such concerns, it is hard to hear the voice of the Lord saying that He "is close to the brokenhearted and saves those who are crushed in spirit" (Psalm 34:18).

I remember all too well how I questioned myself after being diagnosed with clinical depression: *How could this emotional instability have happened? Is it my own fault? Have I brought this frightening, out-of-control feeling on myself by sinning against God?* Oddly enough, in the midst of the self-accusation I was somehow able to see the situation objectively. I recognized that my depressed condition was leading to exaggerated feelings, and that all my searching for sin was an abnormal and self-centered exercise. I simply could not find intentional wrongdoing. The deeper I delved in my search for sin, the more self-absorbed I became. Sometimes I seemed pathetic to myself (and perhaps to others) as I tried to discover possible sins that may have caused God to distance Himself—or so it seemed—from me.

There can be spiritual reasons for depression, which we will discuss later in this chapter. For the moment we are seeking understanding about why Christians who cannot point to a spiritual reason—for example, a sin against God—for still feeling guilty.

Guilty or Not Guilty?

In learning how to deal with guilt and shame, we must start with this: The biblical perspective on life is not a matter of *feeling* guilty; it is a matter of *being* guilty. "All have sinned and fall short of the glory of God" (Romans 3:23). We *are* guilty, whether or not we *feel* guilty. All of us, the whole human race from the beginning to the end of time, are guilty. It is simply a fact.

The Lord Jesus Christ died on the cross as our substitute, punished for our sins and for the sins of the whole world. When we accepted Him as our Savior, it was as if in God's sight we exchanged the dirty rags of our guilt for the immaculate, beautiful robe of Jesus' righteousness. That is what the Bible means when it tells us to "[clothe] yourselves with Christ" (Galatians 3:27). Our act of faith in accepting Christ, inspired and enabled by God Himself, means that the Father sees only the beautiful robe. We were guilty: objective fact. Christ has removed the guilt, and we who believe in Him no longer bear it: objective fact.

But *feeling* guilty before God for that clothing of unrighteousness—that is, recognizing our sinfulness—is something else again. When you and I and all other Christians came to the point of realizing our need for a Savior, we differed in our feelings about that guilt. Some felt deep shame; others responded less intensely. Some of us wept; others of us did not. None of us responded exactly the same, and no person can judge the depth or breadth of the feelings of another. Everyone who has ever run to Christ has done so because the Holy Spirit showed him the fact of his guilt, and not because of his feelings about that guilt.

It is likely, however, that depressed people felt the cutting guilt and shame more deeply—and here is something wonderful. The intensity of their feelings can actually help the depressed see their great need of Jesus as Savior in a way that those who are emotionally stronger may never see. Then the great Healer can help them begin to sort out false guilt from true.

Ultimately, of course, expression of feelings is not the point. Humility is the point. Will we *come* to the Lord Jesus?

What Does It Mean to Be Right with God?

The marvelous exchange of the dirty, ragged clothes of our sin for the clean, beautiful garment of Jesus' righteousness is what theologians call *justification by faith*. It is the basic building block of the Christian life.

As I searched for wrongdoing that could have brought on my depressed condition, I could not come up with deliberate sin against God. I was aware that there were many ways in which I was not what I should be. I failed the Lord often. There were things for which I needed to repent daily, asking for His grace, so that my character would be changed and become more like that of the Lord Jesus. After all, the ultimate will of God for each Christian is that we "be conformed to the likeness of his Son" (Romans 8:29). But deliberate sin I could not find.

It was then that the Bible training I had received in earlier years became a firm rock on which to rest my emotionally tired self. I knew that I must keep returning to the lodestar of the Christian walk: justification by faith.

56

I remember when the liberating joy of this doctrine became real to me. It was about a year after I surrendered my life to the Lord Jesus Christ. My office colleague Kathryn and I were discussing the question of forgiveness of daily sin. How much did we have to keep on asking for forgiveness when, with sincere hearts, we had confessed all known sin to Him? "How sorry can you get?" asked Kathryn, a brand-new Christian.

That conversation those many years ago led me to a book called *The Normal Christian Life* by Chinese Christian Watchman Nee, which was an eye-opener to me. It helped me understand the doctrine of justification by faith for the first time.

Like all spiritual truth, this number-one doctrine needs to be reinforced by regular reading of the Bible and by prayers for understanding and knowledge about how to apply it. It cannot be *discerned* cerebrally, but with the help of the Holy Spirit it must be *applied* cerebrally. No matter how unworthy I felt, or might feel at any time, I was justified. It was "just as if" I had never sinned. I was made right with God forever. I might not feel it now in this depression, I was able to tell myself, but eternal facts were eternal facts.

May I say carefully here that I was given special grace to see this? Not all depressed Christians can. Their emotions are fragile, and it is often difficult for them to claim ownership of the amazing reality of justification on which the whole of Christianity rests.

But isn't it true that even those of us who are well often fail to appropriate the doctrine of justification by faith? Brothers or sisters are heard to say things like, "I'm trying to be a good Christian." How can a Christian say that when it is impossible? Trying to be good never works. We are reckoned good in God's eyes not by our own efforts but by the atoning death of Christ. We glorify God when we believe this gift of grace is true. Only as we appropriate it through the power of the Holy Spirit do we have victory. Sin no longer rules;

God's grace rules. It is imperative that Christians practice this truth. It is the way to live the normal Christian life.

If we know the facts of our justification in the sight of God, our own suffering can be lessened should depression overcome us. I believe mine was, and so was that of my friend Lois.

She is a friend of mine in her fifties, happily married to a businessman. The mother of two young adult daughters, Lois is a mature and balanced Christian, an example I look up to in her practical, warmhearted love for the Lord and for people. She does not have a job outside her home in terms of supplementing the family income, but she loves working hard and spends many hours helping people through her gifts of hospitality and practical servant leadership. Lois is a vivacious adventurer for the Lord.

Not long ago, to her great surprise, Lois was diagnosed with clinical depression. Like me she sought to discover a spiritual reason—for example, willful sin—as a possible cause, but she could not find it. She did not have the sense of darkness, despair, worthlessness and hopelessness that many depressed Christians experience. Her main symptom was deep, unabating fatigue and exhaustion. A teller of vivid stories, Lois described to me one day how difficult it was for her to get up in the mornings. That had not been a problem for me in my own case of depression, and many of us might think that people with this symptom could surely get up if they tried hard enough, but Lois has helped me see how crippling exhaustion can be. When she woke up mornings, she was as tired as when she had gone to bed the night before. She had not received any restorative rest during the night. Her limbs and her back were aching and as heavy as lead. It took extraordinary effort for her just to push back the bed covers.

Over the months since her diagnosis, I have watched Lois respond to her doctor's advice. It has been a refreshing and mature response. She submitted to the diagnosis, obeyed the doctor and sought the Lord, even though it was often hard for her to pray. (Remember, inability to concentrate is a frequent symptom of depression.) But I saw something else tremendously important to her healing. Because Lois knows the Lord and the facts behind her faith in Him, she held onto the teaching of justification by faith that she has applied to her life for decades. And, as I mentioned, Lois has not suffered the dreadful feelings of worthlessness experienced by some Christians.

Could it be that in His plan for Lois' life, God has spared her those feelings? I do not know why many depressed Christians feel abandonment and desolation; no one does except the Lord Jesus. But I do know that Lois has sought to live a life in which she has appropriated by faith and practice the finished work of the Lord Jesus Christ.

Could it be that when a time of crisis comes, and the brain cannot produce normal emotional responses, Christians like Lois can cling to the basic, unchangeable facts of the Christian life? Might we return, like a default setting in a computer, to fact number one, justification by faith, and know that we are right with God?

Christian leaders and mature Christians must keep returning to and emphasizing this basic doctrine without which our faith is in vain. Are we teaching young believers to stand in the truth that there is absolutely nothing we can do to gain right standing with God? Are we living every day in this faith? If we do not practice it, our help to other Christians will be limited. For their sake we must search ourselves and see whether we are appropriating this foundational fact of our faith. And for our own sakes we must appropriate it. Clinical depression can happen to anybody.

Wasn't It Her Fault?

As I have mentioned, I concluded that I could honestly not find deliberate sin in my life. I could not, therefore, say that the depression was my fault. Jesus Christ was my Lord.

Would He not have told me, when I asked Him, if deliberate and willful sin needed to be dealt with? If I felt guilt, then, it had to be false guilt.

But I have also confessed that, before admitting that I belonged in the category of depressed Christians, I felt quite strongly that if a Christian was depressed, it was largely his or her own fault. Surely something in that person's life had not been completely handed over in surrender to the Lord.

I wish I did not have the following example to relate, but I tell it in the hopes that it will enlighten others who feel as I once did.

Anna was a student with long, dark hair who came to visit me at the Intercessory Prayer Ministry office at the university years ago. Anna was in her late twenties, tall and slender. Her face was pretty, but her expression looked anxious. I explained to Anna that I was not a professional counselor and offered to refer her to the university's counseling services. But Anna said she wanted to talk and pray with me about a matter that was troubling her.

She had read the book *Safer than a Known Way,* which I wrote with much joy in 1988. She had traced the story of how, in spite of my fears of being led down a path I did not want to follow, the Lord Jesus helped me make as total a surrender to Him as I knew how to make. She had seen that it was His will to lead me into mission work, even though I had feared that would mean leaving England, speaking in public and being single. And she had seen how it had also been His plan to fulfill my life through the very things I had feared. God's plan did involve my leaving England, learning how to speak in public and remaining single until I was 42 years old.

Anna told me she had done exactly the same thing. She had given her whole life to the Lord—but He had not given to her what she deeply longed and prayed for, a Christian husband. She questioned with some anger why had He had not done so.

I did all I knew to help Anna. We talked about the possibility of unconfessed sin in her life, but she was not aware of any. We talked about the discipline of waiting—after all, she was still a young woman. Or it might be God's plan for her to complete a certain work first, as it had been in my case. Much of my ministry up to that point in my life could never have been carried out wholeheartedly had I not been single. The same could be true in Anna's life, too.

Or, I tried to reason, perhaps it was not the will of God that Anna should ever marry. Marriage is a good thing and is given to most Christians, but it is not given to everybody. If that were the case, was she willing to face it and still follow the Lord?

Anna and I talked and prayed together several times. In spite of my prayers for her and my longing to help her, her attitude did not change. She was angry with God. She had trusted Him with her heart's greatest desire and had not received what she longed for. Apart from this, there was stress in her life for other reasons, and she was finding that stress difficult to deal with.

One day, as I looked at her anxious face during yet another unsuccessful time together, a thought occurred to me.

"You're not depressed, are you?" I asked in surprise.

I can still hear the wording of my query and the incredulous tone in my voice as suspicion dawned that Anna might be depressed. She could not be. That was not possible for a serious Christian.

"Oh, yes, I suppose I am," Anna replied, beginning to weep.

At that time in my thinking, believing depression to be just a spiritual state of mind, this could mean only one thing: There was something Anna had not surrendered to God. It had to be that she had not given Him everything in total submission to His will. If she had, she would not be unhappy and depressed. She would not be questioning God's will. She would not be angry with Him. And I told her so. I hope I did it kindly, but I know I did it definitely, believing that her sadness was of her own making.

I lost touch with Anna after that conversation. Since I had originally told her I was not a professional counselor, and since she was a sensible young woman, I hope she went to see one of the counseling specialists in the psychology department at the university. In any case, I do not recall her coming back to talk to me again.

I know now that my response was not the one I should have given to Anna. After all, she had told me there was nothing in her life that, as far as she knew, had not been committed to God. Perhaps—and this is one of the perplexing questions we must deal with as we seek to help depressed Christians—her depression had so distorted her thinking that anger with God was a response she could not control at that time. Emotional reactions are often magnified in the depressed person. We cannot judge a person's true emotional state. Only God knows.

If I were meeting Anna now, I hope I would recognize more quickly the fact that she was depressed. We are told about the Lord Jesus that "a bruised reed he will not break, and a smoldering wick he will not snuff out" (Isaiah 42:3; Matthew 12:20). The strong, all-knowing One will not further break down a sincere follower who is already weak, nor will He despise the depressed. Remember, "the LORD is close to the brokenhearted and saves those who are crushed in spirit."

How could I have been of real help to Anna? How could I have responded to her as Jesus Christ would have responded? I know depression's crippling effects for myself now and have experienced Jesus' nonjudgmental and kind response. That is how I should have responded to her. But could I have had a more Christlike response without knowing what I now know? Again, of course, I could. A judgmental approach is never the right response of the Christian. We must pray that we will be more like Christ in every aspect of our lives. The Lord can do anything in a follower who humbles herself. Non-depressed Christians can indeed learn. How otherwise will those who are weak through depression receive proper help?

Ten years after my encounter with Anna, it seems to me that depression can occur through any combination of physical, emotional and spiritual reasons. All three parts of our human nature are fallen, and while all are being redeemed (in the words of 2 Corinthians 3:18, "transformed into his likeness"), redemption is a process that will not be completed before Christ's return. Any Christian can experience physical, emotional or spiritual dysfunction without compromising his or her redemption-in-process.

Spiritual Deficiency?

Let's say I had been right in my conclusion that there was something in Anna's life she had not given to the Lord. Let's say there was a spiritual deficiency. After all, she was not coping well with stress, and that could have meant she was not fully trusting God. But that does not mean her experience necessarily involved sin. Even if her depression had resulted from what could rightly be called sin, because there was some exercise of the will involved, I should have remembered my patience with other kinds of sin. What about pride or pretense, for example? I saw these qualities in myself and others, but reasoned that the persons involved were still in the process of being restored to the image of God. Why would I assume that the behavior connected with depression was bigger and darker than those other sins?

Although it would be wrong to minimize a person's responsibility for sin, I can now see that we in the Christian community are in sin ourselves if we exaggerate depressive sins beyond most others, and fail to render compassionate correction in these instances.

And I would now argue that in the case of the committed Christian, most of what the sufferer regards as spiritually

63

based depression results from unintended, rather than deliberate, sin. Our spiritual selves are no less fallen than our physical and emotional selves; there is no more shame in being deficient spiritually than in any other area. We can rightly be impatient with ourselves if our depression involves willful sin, but if it does not, then our condemnation of depression only reveals our impatience with God as He builds His character in us.

For His own good reasons, God designed us to exist within time, and He designed human maturity as a process. The process of sanctification, in which we begin to see our weaknesses as well as our willful disobedience, is not meant to happen all at once; nothing in this world was so designed. It may take more time, for instance, to learn to trust God with some parts of our lives. We might understand mentally that lack of trust in God is, in light of His perfect holiness, sin, but it may take time to see this in ourselves. Babies are not ashamed that they cannot speak yet, nor toddlers that they cannot keep up with politics. So why do we take the full responsibility for the parts of God's time-consuming process that are not accomplished yet?

If being a believer means, primarily, laying oneself open to the process of God reproducing His character in us, then the believer is only one of two participants in the process. We can be ashamed of not submitting to the process, of not facing up to anything that separates us from God, but beyond that, He does the rest and we cannot be ashamed of His action or lack of action.

In fact, the main distinctive of Christianity is that God is the One who does the work, the changing of our character, and not us. All other religions teach that we can and must do it ourselves. Our Lord teaches that we are His workmanship and can only submit to Him. We might not always want to hear about the work He intends to do, but we are dependent on Him to do it because we lack the character or ability to do it ourselves. To take that responsibility wholly on ourselves is what other religions do, and it is errant belief—sin.

So isn't taking on the whole responsibility for what has not changed yet also, in some sense, sin and errant belief? We can take responsibility only for what we have not let God do; we cannot be responsible for what He has not chosen to work on yet.

If a person has not overcome whatever spiritual dimension there might be to his or her depression, we cannot judge whether that person has not allowed God to work, or whether this dimension is only now becoming God's priority for him or her. In fact, the presence of the depression may be a healthy sign that God is starting a new project in that person's life. A more charitable, cooperative, nonjudgmental attitude would serve the Christian community well!

Along with every other serious Christian, I believe 2 Corinthians 5:17: "If anyone is in Christ, he is a new creation; the old has gone, the new has come!" Someone might well argue: "If I am a new creature in Christ, why is the depression not part of the old that has now become new—and therefore fixed?" I truly am a new creation, in the same way that God the Father sees me dressed in the righteousness of His beloved Son, even though I continue to sin. But I still have to deal with the effects of sin in my life while He patiently shows me things He needs to work on in order to reproduce the character of the Lord Jesus in me.

Spiritual Reasons for Depression

Now we discuss spiritual causes for clinical depression—cases in which deliberate sin brought on symptoms so severe that the people involved were unable to function normally.

Not long ago I came to know a young woman named Rebecca. She is a student who heard me speak at a large conference of Christian young people in Louisville, Kentucky, as the year turned from 1994 to 1995. As we talked one day, I told her I was writing a book on depression.

"I want to help people understand that it's not always brought on by deliberate sin," I told Rebecca.

"Yes, that's true," said Rebecca. "But I've just come out of a serious depression myself, and in my case it was indeed caused by sin."

"Can you tell me about it?" I asked.

"I'm embarrassed for you to know what it was," said Rebecca. "But if my story can help others, I'll tell you what happened."

And she did. When she had finished, I asked Rebecca to write out what she had told me and send it to me. Since her story is too long to reproduce in this chapter, I have placed it in Appendix B, "The Desert of Rebellion," on page 181. It is the account of a young woman who confessed her sin to God and was forgiven, restored and healed from depression.

In other cases clinical depression can arise from another spiritual reason—unresolved issues from the past.

Speaking at a conference in California, I came in touch with Cindy, who had suffered for a year from a disabling clinical depression. As far as she knew, there was no deliberate sin in her life, yet there was (as she had learned) a spiritual reason for her depression. As she urgently sought God's healing, He led her to a Christian counselor, who helped Cindy see that she was angry. The root of her anger lay buried in those past traumas that, after her conversion, she had never dealt with. It was only when Cindy faced those difficult issues and forgave those who had hurt or mistreated her that healing came. I will talk more about forgiveness in chapter 9. (Cindy's story appears in Appendix A on page 177.)

I should mention here that another spiritual cause of depression can be satanic oppression. We will discuss this in chapter 6, "Is Depression Satan's Fault?"

How can depressed Christians receive comfort from God, and encouragement and practical help from other Christians?

Before well Christians can help, they must remind themselves that it is never their place to judge the Lord's work in progress in the life of another. Justification by faith alone—that basic building block of the Christian faith—must be the foundation on which the well and the depressed Christian alike stand. Those who have trusted Christ for salvation have indeed become new creatures, which will become evident as they allow God to reproduce the character of His Son in them.

"I try to be a good Christian" can never be part of a believer's vocabulary. It is God and God alone who justifies. Who are we, then, to condemn another? Our loving, practical help, as well as our good example, may be just what are needed to help that person obtain a stronger footing in her or his faith in Christ.

Later we will discuss practical ways in which we can look after the depressed and, therefore, serve them as though we were serving the Lord Jesus Himself. First, though, let's look at another vital building block of the Christian faith. If we do not stand on it firmly, as we stand on justification by faith, we can never know true Christian victory.

Is Depression God's Fault?

Men are not cast off by the Lord forever. Though he brings grief, he will show compassion, so great is his unfailing love. For he does not willingly bring affliction or grief to the children of men.

Lamentations 3:31–33

       When I told about dark-haired Anna in the last chapter, I concluded that I was wrong to make a sweeping generalization that because she was depressed, there must be sin in her life. But there is need for further consideration of one aspect of her story that represents the feelings of many who are depressed.

       Anna declared that she was angry with God. We need to dwell on that difficult subject in this chapter if we are to find or give help in the area of depression. Was Anna right to be angry with God?

"Rights" and the Christian

       Let's talk about the meaning of the word *right*. Derived from Old English, its essence means "straight" or "true." For 25 years I have mainly consulted the *Abridged Oxford Concise Dictionary* when I need to know the meaning of a word. I use large and more modern dictionaries, too, but my old one is portable and has accompanied me to many destinations. Abridged though it is, this small dictionary gives 24 meanings for the word *right,* so I had better define the sense of the word as I use it in this chapter.

Meaning number four in my dictionary, "correct," is the one I am using in the sentence above: Was Anna correct to be angry with God? She was not—but it is important to discuss this step by step.

First we must remind ourselves that the illness of depression causes many people not to be able to reason properly. Their judgment is not always sound or their thinking logical. This may have been the case with Anna. The Lord is patient and kind and will not turn away from those who seek Him, especially those who, because of a fragile emotional state, incorrectly label Him as unfair. That surely is what anger with God implies: He has treated His children unfairly. But God is good and perfect. How can He be unfair?

My next question also contains meaning number 4 of the word *right*. Is it ever right (correct) for a Christian to be angry with God? I refer now to the well Christian, the not-depressed Christian, the one whose emotional state is not fragile but normal. No, it is never correct for that person to be angry with God either. I do not mean we cannot be angry with God. Of course we can. But we cannot be angry with God *righteously*.

It is now the turn of meaning number sixteen of *right*. In this sense *right* means "entitlement" or "fair claim." Does a Christian have any rights at all in this sense? Not according to Scripture. It teaches us that all our gain should be counted loss for the sake of Christ; that indeed we have no rights at all. In Philippians 3:7–8 the apostle Paul says: "Whatever was to my profit I now consider loss for the sake of Christ. What is more, I consider everything a loss compared to the surpassing greatness of knowing Christ Jesus my Lord."

I do not mean there are not certain civil rights that we can be afforded as citizens of a nation. Paul used his rights as a Roman citizen to appeal his case at least twice. Some modern countries place great importance on the rights of their citizens, which are spelled out in their charters. These are temporal and human rights and must sometimes be given up if they could bring harm to others. Paul also wrote about having the right, humanly speaking, to be married, but he had forfeited that right for the sake of the Gospel. In the final analysis everything a Christian might perceive as a right needs to be relinquished to Christ. We have no rights, except to the Lord Jesus Christ, and by the free gift of God's grace we have every right to Him.

As a young woman I was much influenced by the life of Amy Carmichael, who spent most of her life for the sake of reaching India with the Gospel; and by the life and death of Jim Elliot, whose statement "He is no fool who gives what he cannot keep to gain what he cannot lose" was proved by martyrdom in the jungles of Ecuador. Both these Christians showed me that all must be surrendered to the Lord Jesus. I longed to prove the all-sufficiency of Christ just as they had. And I did prove it. As a young woman I laid down all rights as far as I understood them. It was the hardest thing I have ever done, and I must admit I did it with tears.

Among those rights was the right to happiness. God often gives happiness, and joy is a fruit of His Holy Spirit, but happiness is nobody's *right*. God has never promised it. If a Christian believes that happiness is his or her right, and then experiences unhappiness, that person might conclude that God is being unfair by allowing the unhappiness, and that blaming God is therefore an appropriate response. But it is never appropriate. God is not unfair. How can it then be right to blame Him?

Being Angry at the Right Things

Because nothing can happen outside the control of God, some would say that He is the correct focus of anger when life deals cruel and unfair blows. But we need to look at some distinctions.

Is it wrong to be angry? Of course not. God Himself urges us to be so. In Ephesians 4:26 He tells us to "be angry but do not sin" (RSV). *Be angry* in the Greek appears in the imperative case. It is a command. We are told to be angry. It is normal and right to be angry at sin, at the results of sin (in circumstances that cause suffering) and at Satan. But it is not right to be angry with God.

Let me say again that a believer, when in shock and anguish and disbelief, may well be angry with God. I recall Carmen and her family. Twenty-five years ago her thirteen-year-old son Peter committed suicide. Nobody had anticipated the tragedy because Peter seemed to be his normal self. His close Christian family was devastated at the violent, self-inflicted ending to his life. Before long anger set in. The family members were angry with themselves, with each other, with Peter, with his schoolteachers and with anybody who could have prevented the suicide. That included God who, in His mercy, most surely did not turn away from them.

Although anger with Him is never appropriate (because He cannot be unfair), its expression in such cases is understandable. Yet I remember the response of another Christian whose husband was killed in the crash of a light aircraft. Her first words on hearing of the accident were: "The Lord gives, and the Lord takes away. Blessed be the name of the Lord."

Consider the perfect nature of God. It is one of goodness and love. God is always perfectly good and cannot be otherwise. The psalmist writes, "You are good, and what you do is good" (Psalm 119:68). This does not just mean God does good things. It also means He can never do bad things. All He does is good, always. Our faith depends completely on

71

the goodness of God. If God did bad things, it would be foolish to trust Him. The basis of our faith is that God is good and that He always acts in a way that is good for His children. Faith can say things that reason can never say. "It was good for me to be afflicted," says Psalm 119:71, "so that I might learn your decrees."

Let's ask the Lord for help in seeing that anger with Him is not appropriate for His children. If you are angry with God, tell Him so. Such a prayer might be worded like this: "Lord, I'm angry with You. I know I shouldn't be, but I am. I need Your help in straightening this out."

King David was angry with God, even in the face of sin. Second Samuel 6 tells of the transporting of the Ark of the Covenant, the symbol of God's presence, by oxcart to Jerusalem. God had instructed, however, that the Ark itself was not to be touched but was to be carried only by poles inserted into rings on the sides of the chest (see Exodus 25:12–14). When the oxen pulling the cart stumbled, Uzzah reached out his hand to steady the Ark and was struck dead. "Then David was angry because the LORD's wrath had broken out against Uzzah" (2 Samuel 6:8).

David must have known that, by touching the Ark, which was the holiest of all the objects in the Tabernacle, Uzzah had transgressed a clear command of God. We are not told how long David remained angry or just how his anger was resolved. Taken at face value, this incident seems to be but a blip on the radar screen of David's walk with God. He must have come to see what had happened from God's viewpoint and repented of his anger, for the story continues, showing David—after a little while— in high celebration, bringing the Ark into Jerusalem.

We should not feel guilty at being angry with God as long as we acknowledge that it is inappropriate. God dealt kindly and patiently with David when he acknowledged his anger. God deals kindly and patiently with us, too, when we acknowledge our anger at Him.

When we humble ourselves and submit to God, He helps us be appropriately angry—that is, angry at the right things. And the result of a humbled and quieted heart is that the Lord can show us some of the reasons for the suffering that has made us angry.

Understanding Suffering

The effects of sin in our imperfect world are pain and suffering, and God in His sovereignty has not chosen to deliver His children from these effects. This book is not the place to try to fathom the mystery of suffering in any depth, but I think of a specific prayer of Corrie ten Boom's through which she was eventually shown at least part of the reason for her suffering. Tante (Dutch for "Aunt") Corrie, for whom I worked for the seven years prior to her death in 1983, lost several family members in the Holocaust of World War II. She prayed: "Lord, help me to see my suffering from Your point of view."

The result of that prayer was that she helped thousands of people all over the world to forgive their enemies. During the last five years of her life, Corrie ten Boom suffered successive strokes that paralyzed and silenced her. In that difficult time I set myself to try to understand more about suffering. I knew that Christians through the ages had plumbed suffering's depths, and that my own quest might reveal nothing new. But perhaps there were fresh insights to be gained at the mysterious and silent end of the life of one of the greatest Christian women communicators that God has given to His Church in our time.

Yet although I sought these insights intently, I learned that there are no depths to suffering that human beings have not already plumbed. Through the centuries many Christians who accepted pain and suffering as mysterious realities allowed by God—although they did not understand them—drew close to Him. And many who did not accept pain and

73

suffering and who blamed God for them did not have peace and did not help others find peace.

Time has helped me see pain as a gift of life. Without it we would not feel. We would not seek God. We would not receive His comfort. And we would never experience the mystery that our most intensely distressing times can also be times of deepest fellowship with God—if we accept the suffering as allowed by Him for ultimate good. The paradox is that peace in pain and suffering lies in accepting them, not in seeking to eradicate them.

We cannot experience that paradox, however, unless we lay down our perceived right to be happy and comfortable. Faith has to come before understanding. And our understanding of the meaning of pain is still only partial. God has not chosen to reveal the whole mystery. He is God. He can reveal what He wants to reveal. That is His right.

A Lesson from Amy Carmichael

As an adult in Dohnavur, India, Amy Carmichael could say it was a good thing she had brown eyes. But as a child in Ireland, she had very much wanted blue eyes. She had heard at church that God answers prayer, and she prayed often that He would change the color of her eyes. One night her prayers were particularly intense. She was sure, as she closed them in sleep, that in the morning her eyes would be blue. But when she awoke and checked in the mirror, she looked into eyes that were as brown as ever. God did not give Amy what she wanted and she was disappointed.

Years later, however, when she was dressed as an Indian woman with only her eyes unveiled, in order to rescue children from enforced temple prostitution, she was glad her eyes were not blue. That would have betrayed her identity and she could not have continued her rescue work. As a mature person she understood why her prayers as a child had not been answered.

It is the same with many Christians of our generation. I refer to those who are well and whom God wants to use to help the depressed. Our culture encourages us to show emotion, especially anger. But anger with God is not the mark of a strong Christian, rather of an immature Christian. One of the principal privileges of the Christian is to declare the goodness of God and to affirm that fact to those who are depressed and who, with unstable emotions, may not be able to affirm it themselves. "We who are strong ought to bear with the failings of the weak and not to please ourselves" (Romans 15:1).

Amy Carmichael expressed her submission to the will of God and her trust in His goodness in a poem that I have read time and again through the years. When I was in Africa, for example, on my first mission assignment and feeling very homesick. When I was nearing forty, still single in the Lord's service and coming to realize I would never have the children I had always wanted. And when my husband was diagnosed with malignancy. The poem is called "In Acceptance Lieth Peace." Its writer tries first to forget sorrow, then to fill life with activity, then to withdraw from life, then to resign herself to the sorrow, before finally finding peace through accepting the circumstances.

I never saw Corrie ten Boom express anger with God during the seven years I worked for her, even during nearly five years of serious illness.

One Christian I talked with about anger toward God expressed his thinking this way: "Oh, God is big enough to take on any anger we feel or express toward Him." While this is true—of course, He is big enough—that does not make it right ever to be angry with God or to complain to Him.

"Master!" cried the disciples, whose fishing boat was at the point of capsizing on stormy Lake Galilee while Jesus slept in the bow. "Don't You care that we are about to die?"

Don't You care? These must be some of the most cutting words in the Bible! Who has ever cared more than Jesus has?

Life is not as it should be. Life is grossly unfair. It was not the original plan of God for there to be such inequality, such pain. But God is not unfair. A great reckoning will come one day. The last shall be first and the first last. In the meantime there are many instances when we must simply accept life. Railing against its unfairness can prolong recovery from depression and impede our maturity in Christ.

The Appropriate Response When Bad Things Happen

The first chapter of 1 Samuel tells of the painful events that led to the birth of the great prophet Samuel, the one chosen by God to anoint the first kings of Israel. Elkanah, who lived in the hill country of Ephraim, had two wives—Hannah, who had no children, and Peninnah, who had several. In a time when a woman's worth was closely related to the number of children she bore, Hannah was miserable. And because Elkanah loved Hannah rather than Peninnah, Hannah's rival taunted her "in order to irritate her" (verse 6).

Each year Elkanah went to worship the Lord and to sacrifice to Him at Shiloh. On one of these trips, when Elkanah took the whole family with him, Hannah went by herself to the Temple to pray. That day was destined to be a momentous one in her life. Her prayers (even though God does not always answer prayers in the direct way He answered Hannah's) can help us know the appropriate response to Him in times of anguish.

We are told that Hannah wept much before God "in bitterness of soul" (verse 10). She pleaded with Him that she might be given a son. She promised God that if He would grant her request, she would give the boy back to Him for his whole life.

Hannah persevered in her prayer at the Temple that day, not speaking aloud but forming the words with her lips. Eli the priest, sitting on a chair at the doorway of the Temple, watched her and assumed she was drunk. He told her so. But Hannah protested that she was not drunk; rather, that she had been pouring out her soul to the Lord in great anguish and grief.

You and I can do that, too. Without railing against Him, we can take our grief, sorrow and "bitterness of soul" to the Lord and pour them out to Him in prayer.

Hannah's response to God was an honest one. She did not try to hide her feelings from Him. Nor should we. It is not normal for Christians to walk stoically through loss and not be honest with God about our grief and desperation. He wants us to express to Him our unhappiness and anger at the unfairness of life. We can describe the circumstances (although He already knows them) without anger at Him. We might begin by saying, "Lord, this is terrible. I don't understand." As we do, let us be sure to mix our sorrow with faith in God.

Christians who are depressed are sometimes unable to concentrate for long in prayer. If this is true of you, simply do what you can. Just come to Him. If your mind is circling too wildly to think, reason or pray, perhaps all you will be able to say is, "Lord, help." I want to ask you to come not with anger in your heart and mind at Him—but if that is the only way you can come, come anyway. He will not turn you away. Bring faith with you, even if it is not very much.

The sovereignty of God, like justification by faith that we talked about in the last chapter, is a basic building block of the Christian faith. If the Christian who has not known depression asks God to help her see things from His point of view, she may one day be in a stronger position to help those who are depressed. If the Christian who has never been depressed submits to loss as allowed by a supremely loving Lord, he may one day be in a stronger position not only to help others, but also to keep a more even perspective should depression ever come to him. Unless Christians, well or depressed, have a proper view of the sovereignty of God— that He can do anything He wants with our lives and we will still trust Him—we can never live truly victoriously.

Believers who are not depressed but want to reach out to those who are must ask the Lord to help them develop and hold onto a high view of His sovereignty. God can use even us to help those for whom illness and loss have brought a very narrow focus to life, including the tendency to blame God. It is the responsibility of those who are strong to help the weak by proclaiming and displaying the constant goodness of God. Those who are angry with God when uncomfortable things happen are in a dangerous position. Their mentality could become that of a victim. A victim can never be a victorious Christian because he or she does not take personal responsibility for anything. It is always someone else's fault when things go wrong or bad things happen.

Let's pray that Christians in our day will gain a much higher view of the sovereignty of God—not a fatalistic resignation, but vibrant faith that a loving and faithful God allows even the most devastating losses for an eventually good purpose. Let's practice proclaiming His goodness and watching for it every moment of our lives. The well Christian will be better equipped to help the ill Christian if a healthy view of God's right to do what He likes in our lives prevails. And should depression one day come to the well Christian, a high view of God's sovereignty might help healing take place more quickly. It is worth repeating that anger with God can extend the agony of depression and delay healing.

In this chapter I have tried to emphasize the goodness and loving nature of God. It is not right to be angry with Him who made us and who has every right to allow whatever He ordains in the lives of His children, for it will ultimately be for His glory and therefore our good. This sometimes means that He allows us or our loved ones to suffer depression. While the Christian cannot be righteously angry with God, he or she can and should be angry at sin and its resulting worldwide pain and loss.

On our journey so far, we have discussed whether depression is the fault of the person suffering from it, and whether it is the fault of God. What about Satan? How much blame should he get?

Is Depression Satan's Fault?

... Lest Satan should take advantage of us; for we are not ignorant of his devices.

2 Corinthians 2:11, NKJV

After speaking at a conference in the heartland of America, I heard from a woman named Carol:

> My mother-in-law, Susan, has had problems with depression, and puts so much guilt on herself, feeling responsible for it and believing that Christians shouldn't be depressed. She tends to focus on Satan and the spiritual battle, attributing all of it to Satan. My husband and I believe that this response is not healthy. I wonder how many other Christians do the same? I hate to see her focusing on Satan and what he is doing, rather than on God and what He is doing. I hope you are able to address this in your book.

Having concentrated in the previous chapter on the magnificent character of

God, perhaps this is the place to consider the despicable character of Satan and what role, if any, he plays in depression. Who is he, really? And does he figure in the depression equation?

Satan is a Hebrew word signifying an adversary, an enemy, an accuser. We must remember that Satan is a created being, not simply a malignant spiritual influence or force. He is also a fallen being with legions of evil spirits or demons at his command. One of the mysteries of the Christian faith is that Satan is allowed so much power. Though he was defeated at the cross (see Colossians 2:13–15) and will be thrown forever into the lake of fire (see Revelation 20:10), for now he exercises tremendous influence. He is described in the Bible as a "roaring lion" (1 Peter 5:8), "the god of this age" (2 Corinthians 4:4), "the ruler [prince] of the kingdom of the air" (Ephesians 2:2).

The Three Facets of the Devil's Identity

Satan has a mission and purpose that Jesus summed up succinctly in ten words: "The thief comes only to steal and kill and destroy" (John 10:10).

These three descriptive verbs can serve as a basis for discovering Satan's devices: *steal, kill, destroy*. There is, it appears, a progressive nature to his actions. He steals in order to kill, and ultimately to destroy. Without giving Satan any respect or too much attention, let's work out what his devices are so that we might watch for them.

A Thief

How may it be said that Satan "steals"? Do you remember the parable of the sower in Matthew 13? Jesus taught that as soon as some of the good seed is sown, the birds, which represent the devil in the parable, snatch up the seeds and gobble them up. The devil tries to steal God's Word from the human heart, lest a person believe and be delivered from Satan's grasp.

The devil is the ultimate killjoy. He tempts and deceives and trips us up. We fall into miserable guilt and are thus robbed of our joy. He also steals our affections from God. That is what happened in the Garden, when he stole the hearts of Adam and Eve away from their Creator.

A Murderer

Jesus also said that Satan is "a murderer from the beginning" (John 8:44). The sworn enemy of the triune God and the inciting force behind the murder of the Messiah, Satan has been venting his hateful wrath on the human race for thousands of years. This seems to be his way of getting back at God. We have recently ended the twentieth century and stepped into a new millennium. And in the century just past, millions of Christians were persecuted and killed—more than in all the previous nineteen centuries combined!

Not only Christians have been murdered. In the Holocaust alone, six million Jewish lives were taken. Satan, the murderer, is behind this wanton slaughter.

At the beginning of the book of Job, Satan was giving a report to God of his wanderings to and fro on the earth. The Lord pointed with pride to Job and asked Satan if he had observed that righteous man. Satan contended that Job was good for good reason: God had blessed him and everything his fingers touched. "But stretch out your hand and strike everything he has, and he will surely curse you to your face," the devil dared Him (Job 1:11).When God gave Satan permission to test Job, ultimately bringing that righteous man to a better place and a deeper understanding of His Maker, Satan immediately brought on the deaths of all seven of Job's sons and all three of his daughters. The only reason he did not murder Job himself was that God had not given him permission to do so. What an insight into the brutal character of our spiritual adversary!

I am sure that if we could see behind the scenes of the murders, assassinations, terrorist slaughters and suicides of our day, we would see Satan's form lurking.

A Destroyer

In what ways is Satan a destroyer?

Postmodern man looks at the destruction that has happened in history, which is increasingly a part of life today, and blames God—"if there is a God." Indeed, the Bible does use the word *destroy* many times to speak of God's activities. But that is not the whole story. God, who is holy and who made us for Himself, will not allow Satan, the real destroyer, unbridled rule.

Though it may appear that God is vengeful, capriciously using and abusing His power, He is always working for good, for the redemption of the world. In the end that will be clear. God does not destroy human lives with drugs. He does not destroy marriages with lies. He does not destroy the good that humans can create on earth. No, those are the works of Satan.

The Devil and Depression

Well, then, is the devil in the details of depression? In our all-too-brief look at his ways, is there reason to blame Satan?

Has anything been stolen from the depressed? Certainly joy has been stolen. As I noted early in this book, sadness is one of depression's frequent companions.

The depressed have also suffered the loss of their vitality. Many people suffering from depression sleep their days away, and thus are also robbed of a happy, productive life. Fear, which accompanies many cases of depression, is present because a person's peace has been stolen. If it is Satan's nature to steal, it seems reasonable that he has played a part in these thefts.

Has depression caused anyone's death or destruction? The question hardly needs asking.

Rebecca, the student about whom I wrote in chapter 4, exemplifies Satan's promotion of physical destruction. She is the young woman who realized her depression had its source in sin and whose fuller testimony appears in Appendix B. Rebecca told me that during her depression, surprising ideas would come to her in dreams at night—clever ideas about ways to commit suicide so that nobody would ever guess her death was not an accident. Such dreams have Satan's nasty fingerprints all over them. Rebecca was able to resist the temptation to end her life, although Satan, seeing she was weak and vulnerable, tried to use her weakness and vulnerability to destroy her.

He always uses the same tricks. Paul writes in the Scripture at the head of this chapter that "we are not ignorant of his devices." Neither should we be. We must remember that Satan is constantly at work. He deceives, distracts, manipulates and works hard to keep Christians in unforgiveness, and he uses any situation to gain a foothold in forwarding his destructive goals. We have no need to fear him, but we must not be naïve about his activity in our world.

Thus we see evident links between Satan and depression. But since depression has many causes and, in fact, comes in most cases from a combination of causes, is it right to attribute it all to Satan?

The main cause of Rebecca's depression was deliberate sin. Satan, by virtue of her rebellion, was given access to her life and made things worse. Voluntary sin always provides an opening for the devil because it separates us from God and from His protection.

And there may be isolated instances in which individuals suffer from depression solely because of demonic attack or oppression. Part of the baffling mystery is that these attacks, as far as we can tell, are unrelated to events in their lives. In some families there appears to be satanic oppression over several generations. Corrie ten Boom discussed this kind of spiritual warfare in her little booklet *Defeated Enemies*. (See the information about this and other recommended resources at the end of this book.)

I want to be ever so careful here. None of us has cause to point a finger. We live in a fallen world, and even the children of God suffer the consequences of mankind's rebellion against Him. As we have discussed in chapter 4, however, we must examine ourselves, if overtaken by depression, to ask if somehow personal sin has given an opening to the enemy. It is wrong, however, to leap to the conclusion that sin in our lives or in others' lives is the cause.

"All Discouragement Is of the Devil"

In talking about Rebecca, I said that the devil tried to take advantage of her, "seeing she was weak and vulnerable." This is surely one of Satan's most common devices. Remember that he will take advantage of any weakness and try to use it toward his goal of total destruction.

When I say that the depressed Christian is often weak, I do not mean that his or her character is inferior to that of other Christians. I mean that this Christian has been brought down physically and emotionally by a debilitating illness. Satan loves to use this vulnerability, if possible, to bring spiritual destruction as well.

He attempts to whip us when we are down. He is merciless and without pity. His spirit is the opposite of that of Christ. Satan loves breaking bruised reeds and snuffing out smoking flax. On the one hand he is clever in a devious way; on the other, stupid.

When did Satan mount his first major attack on Jesus? It was after Jesus had fasted for forty days in the wilderness. Being weak, hungry and alone, Jesus appeared a good target. It is useful to us, in learning how to counteract the devil, to consider the way Jesus handled the devil's temptations. He did not try to reason with Satan or to deny his existence. Rather He resorted to the Word of God: "It is written . . . it is written . . . it is written."

One of the devil's most useful tools is *discouragement*. Someone has said, "All discouragement is of the devil." Lorne Sanny wrote when he was president of The Navigators:

> Beware of the discourager. One of Satan's most effective measures is to break our spirit. A discouraged or a heavy spirit is an infectious thing. It sweeps across people like Asian flu. The war in which we are engaged is neglected. The promises God has made are forgotten. That which God means for us to possess remains in the hand of the enemy.

What the Scripture describes of Elijah, a discouraged saint in the Bible, is borne out in our own human experience. After the exultation of victory on Mount Carmel, where he fearlessly faced down 450 false prophets, he sank into abject gloom over Queen Jezebel's threats. We, too, are susceptible to discouragement after spiritual highs. But the remedy for Elijah was not primarily a spiritual prescription. No, the angel who visited him invited him to eat and drink and rest (see 1 Kings 19:5–9). He did not need to deal with sin; he simply needed to take special care of himself.

So may we in our depression—and so may we encourage our depressed brother or sister.

Depression and
Modern Times

My times are in your hands.

Psalm 31:15

Few would deny that technological advances, while often beneficial, have also quickened the pace of our lives in a way that has not always been for the better. The speeding up of our world has brought confusion, especially to older members of society, and a more competitive edge to businesses large and small, with companies downsizing and outsourcing. Many individuals have become increasingly isolated behind computers. Most of us will agree that these and many other factors in our modern times have caused us increased stress.

And too much stress often leads to depression.

What is stress? "A constraining or impelling force; effort, demand upon energy," says my *Concise Oxford Dictionary*.

The physiological definition of stress includes a real or per-ceived threat, the release of hormones to aid fight-or-flight, and muscles poised for action. The problem occurs when the stress response is turned on too often, as this increases the likelihood of both physical and psychological difficulties. When I went to live in the Netherlands in 1968 to work with Brother Andrew ("God's Smuggler" of Bibles to Communist coun-tries) and his team, my first challenge was to learn the Dutch language. Because many of the Dutch speak English well, I soon realized I would never learn their language unless my work colleagues and new friends agreed not to speak English to me except when they had to explain something important. They did so, and during my first couple of months in Holland, I tried to train myself to hear the language.

Before long I could pick out several words that were fre-quently part of normal conversation. It was as if they kept rising to the top of the new sounds in my brain. I reckoned they must be important because of the number of times they were repeated, not just at work but at the grocery store, at church, on the television news and in the homes of friends. And it seemed to me that two of these words were used more often than others: *mensen* (people) and *spanning* (stress).

If frequent word use suggests the importance of what those words represent, then *mensen* and *spanning* held top-ranking positions in the lives of the Dutch. They did, of course, and not only because Holland is one of the world's most densely populated countries. People are obviously the most important element in any society and, if my Dutch-learning observation holds true, then *stress* is closely connected to *people*.

Relationships with people are often difficult, and you do not have to live very long to prove it. Our friend Rick had this exchange one Sunday morning with his two-year-old son, who was reluctant to get dressed.

"What will your friends at church think if you don't wear a shirt today?" he asked.

"I hate my friends!" replied little Nathan.

Apparently stress in relationships begins early.

More than three decades have passed since I learned Dutch, but ever since then, even in English, *people* and *stress* have held a special connection for me. None of us, even the most shy and the least influential, goes through life without inter-acting with and influencing many other people. I am a little surprised that *spanning* (stress) entered so frequently into conversations in Holland many years ago; I wonder how often I would hear it if I were learning Dutch today. I also wonder what today's learners of English hear. I suspect that the word *depression*, rarely part of conversation thirty years ago, is now in regular use. This is good, not because the disease is more common but because it is at least being talked about.

The world has widened for us and at the same time become smaller. Many of us must relate to more people than we had to even a decade ago, and nearly all of us have to relate to more people than our grandparents would have imagined possible. But that relating is often transitory and superficial.

Many of us have too much stress in our lives, and that can result in emotional overload. What steps can we take to reduce stress? In this chapter I present seven ways that are sure to help:

Understand the times in which we live.
Know that this is God's time for you.
Simplify your life.
Find ways to regain perspective.
Discover the art of strolling.
Learn to wait.
Hold plans lightly.

Understand the Times in Which We Live

The Old Testament records for us that among the soldiers who joined King David's army at Hebron were certain "men

88

of Issachar, who understood the times" (1 Chronicles 12:32). We must pray for understanding of our own times and the part that depression plays in them. The Lord will give us this understanding if we ask Him for it. He can lead us to information and give us spiritual insight to help us understand.

Our discernment will be limited, of course, but let's ask Him earnestly to teach us what we need to know. You may gain one perspective about depression, and I another, but together we Christians must work toward better understanding of the problem. Just think how good and blessed it will be when we live together in closer harmony through deeper understanding! Surely we will then be much more effective in reaching the depressed who do not yet know the Lord.

One of the ways God has answered my prayer for clearer understanding of our modern times has been to help me step back and view part of the bigger picture. On a larger stage of life than the one my daily life presents, I can see three giants struggling together. Although we usually do not spend much time consciously contemplating their struggle, these three giants affect our thinking and our actions as ordinary Christians.

The giants' names are *Theology, Existential Philosophy* and *Medicine*. One does not need to be a theologian, philosopher or medical scientist to see how these giants are affecting us, by virtue of their power over our world. In fact, these giants can make it difficult for Christians to accept depression in themselves, much less to seek treatment.

Giant #1: Theology

Christian theology—literally, "a word about God," or the study of God—has been developed over the past two thousand years. For my daily life, a handy summary of vital doctrine is contained not only in the Apostles' Creed but also in a chorus, "One Day!" by J. Wilbur Chapman, that I learned in Sunday school:

89

Living, He loved me;
Dying, He saved me;
Buried, He carried my sin far away!
Rising He justified
Freely, forever.
One day He's coming,
O glorious day!

I love that song and repeat it in my mind. Carey and I sing it together sometimes.

Christians have many vital doctrines to meditate on, all of them worked out from Scripture through the centuries under the guidance of the Holy Spirit. We need the grounding of biblical theology more than ever in this third millennium. Although the setting on the stage of life has changed, God still wills that Christians live with victory and joy in the present and with the hope of heaven at the end of our earthly journeys.

But what about depressed people who do not display victory, joy and hope in their lives, and who are so overwhelmed that they are unable to derive purpose and meaning from their faith? How does depression relate to human responsibility and personal sin, given its biochemical connection and frequent responsiveness to medication? How does depression relate to God's sovereignty? To our spiritual adversary?

Theology is our lifeline in a troubled world. But our biblical understanding of depression is inadequate, as the giant of theology in this post-Christian era must grapple with other giants on the stage of life.

Giant #2: Existential Philosophy

Our times are no longer thoroughly influenced by the idea of God. The philosophies of recent centuries have led to strongly secular thinking. The prevailing philosophy of our day is existentialism, the second giant on today's stage.

Existentialism says that life is meaningless and purposeless. There is no absolute truth; truth is relative. Individuals should make decisions on the basis of what seems right at the time. Enjoyment of the moment is what counts, even if that brings discomfort to others.

Because immediate enjoyment or relief by whatever means possible is paramount in the modern world, and because drug use is rampant, some concerned Christians strongly resist the use of any therapies or medicines that might be considered quick fixes. They see these as part of the encroachment of the spirit of our day, existential philosophy, on Christianity.

Giant #3: Medicine

A third oversized player on the stage of life today is medical science. In His grace God has answered many prayers for the treatment of disease. Men and women are living longer than they have since the days of Noah. Research, information and knowledge have burgeoned, including in the area of mental illness. We know now that there are real, measurable reasons for depression. Researchers have learned that when the brain has insufficient levels of certain neurotransmitters—the chemicals that allow brain cells to communicate with each other—depressive symptoms result.

Although medication is not always the answer for those suffering from depression, I believe it often needs to be part of the treatment. Some Christians disagree. Faith in the Lord Jesus should be enough, they argue. The way of the world—the prevailing philosophy of existentialism—is to do whatever makes a person feel better. Thus, they say, if a Christian takes antidepressant medication, he or she is simply caught up in the current "quick-fix, feel-better" mindset of the non-Christian (although the same philosophy does not hold true for taking aspirin or pain relievers).

Seeking Insight into the Age

So what can we do in our thinking and perception to reduce stress and depression? First we can ask God to give us understanding of our times. When I did that, He helped me step back and see a bigger part of the picture. I offer my simple description of the three giants as an example of a way in which the Lord can give us understanding of our times if we ask Him.

Some Christians are not willing to think much about the clash of theology, prevailing philosophy and medical science. For years I, too, found the relationship among the three too daunting to investigate. What if looking at them too closely somehow undermined Christianity?

But there is no need to be afraid of that. We have a living Lord, and the better I get to know Him, the surer I become that He is Lord of history, of developing thought and of scientific breakthroughs. He will look after His own glory—and He will look after His own children, including those in depression. As those of us who are well seek better understanding and insight, our Lord will show us how to care for our generation with patience and kindness.

Know That This Is God's Time for You

Another way to prevent stress and depression is to remember that this is the time in which it was ordained that you and I should live.

Some years ago somebody made the playful remark to me that I was the kind who could have coped much better with life if I had been born a hundred years earlier. "You were not made to travel faster than the speed of horses!" he added.

Looking back, I find this an interesting insight into my low toleration of stress. But there is no point in contemplating whether life might have been easier for us in a different time period. The truth is that God, in His sovereignty and will, determined that you and I should be born on the dates on which we were born and not at any other time. "All the days ordained for me were written in your book before one of them came to be" (Psalm 139:16).

And since He promises to care for His children, it follows that God has grace available for you and me to live at the time in which we are living. No fate or accident determined the days of our births. Our loving God did. He wants our lives to glorify His name in this day. That glory will be largely reflected in how we Christians love—and therefore help— each other in a world that is constantly outpacing itself.

"Stop the world, I want to get off" was a catch phrase in the 1970s. The phrase always reminded me of the merry-go-round with big wooden horses that came to our town when the fair visited every year. As a child I feared its speed and was glad when the ride was over. Now it seems to me as if this planet is hurtling out of control through space and time, gathering speed. There is no way to stop it so that I can disembark. Since God sustains all His creation, it is better that we seek to view the apparent speed of the world from His perspective—but I must admit that, yes, sometimes the Victorian age is an attractive one for me!

But it was not God's century for me, and as I hold this truth central in my life, I am given a little more of His point of view. And that reduces stress and depression.

Are there more ways to reduce them?

Simplify Your Life

Speaking of Victorians, I am reminded of a week in November 1984 that turned out to be one of the most fascinating of my life. A year after the death of Corrie ten Boom I began my writing career by receiving guidance from two respected Christian narrative authors. John and Elizabeth Sherrill, writers of *The Hiding Place* and other true stories

93

that have had wide and deep effects on our generation, showed me how to improve my account of the unusual end of Tante Corrie's life. The book was published under the title *The Five Silent Years of Corrie ten Boom*.

One of the first things I learned was that modern-day storytelling requires concise writing. But this has not always been the case. Victorian readers in the time of Charles Dickens loved his long and sometimes rambling stories with their wordy preambles. They were just right for long summer days outside and cold winter nights by the fireside. It is not surprising to learn that Dickens and other writers of his time were paid by the word! For some families there was a lot of time for reading, and in the average household not many other pastimes competed with the book.

But times change. My writing instructors in 1984 warned me that, given all the competition reading has these days, I could not indulge in preamble and wordiness. My story had to be told with strict economy of words. If I wanted my book to be read, I needed to capture the attention of the readers on page one. I would probably not have another chance to regain it. Consider a quick list of some of the attractions at that time that competed for the hours that might be spent reading a book: the car, the television, movies, 24-hour supermarkets, the mall, the telephone.

Now that the century has turned, we can add many more items: computers, electronic games, the Internet, e-mail, videos. We have many more choices open to us on how we spend our time, and we appear to have less time than ever.

Obviously the number and variety of options facing us can heighten stress. So take stock often. In what ways are you using your energy and time? Ask for the Holy Spirit's help in recognizing where you are spending time unnecessarily and where stress is being compounded. And once He has shown you, be brave enough to ask Him for the strength to take definite steps to simplify your life.

When life becomes simpler, marvelous de-stressors previously obscured by hurry and clutter become focused and visible against the backdrop of life. Simplifying reduces stress.

Find Ways to Regain Perspective

In 1998 Carey and I took a large step to simplify our lives. We moved from noisy, busy, metropolitan Dallas/Fort Worth to a much quieter place, a rural area of Waxahachie about thirty miles southeast.

One of the results of this move, a tremendous gift from God to me and a large part of my own healing from depression, is the regaining of perspective and a new view of who is really in control of our times. From God's perspective we are not stuck on fast forward.

Although the drive to and from our daily work is now twice as long, Carey and I find that the benefits of living in the country far outweigh the longer commute. Life has slowed down. Grocery shopping has to be better planned since I cannot just run out to the store when I have forgotten to buy milk. It is calming to see the progress of Carey's vegetable garden. As I watch the plants grow in their measured way, my soul slows down. I remember that waiting is an important part of life.

And the sky! As a child I read a poem called "Under an English Heaven," but now I live under a Texas heaven, and it is beautiful. Rarely have I seen a bigger sky. City lights do not hinder the view at night, and it is full of jewels for most of the year.

Last evening Carey and I sat on our dark blue easy chairs, each reading sections of the *Dallas Morning News*. He told me he had just read that Mars was in a particularly good spot for viewing, so he got up, opened the door to the back porch, went outside and searched the sky for the red planet. It is now as normal for us to view the heavens as it is to put the kettle on for a cup of tea. Carey found Mars just where the paper said it would be, and came in again and resumed his reading.

This is a small example, perhaps, but it comforts me to know that Mars is exactly where it should be. God who sustains the universe makes sure of that. And if Mars is just where it should be, so is planet earth. You and I are sustained just as firmly. Nothing lies outside God's control.

Regaining our perspective through considering His handiwork is vital to the health of His children. Not everyone can move to the countryside, but most of us can find ways to spend more time outdoors in the fresh air in beautiful places. Not only do we gain better perspective, but we often acquire an instinctive assurance as well—almost a "remembering." Is this because we humans made in the image of God have an innate longing for unfettered worship—the really true perspective that we lost when Adam fell and that one day will be thoroughly restored? This is the Christian's greatest hope, and the more we keep it in mind, the healthier we will be.

Discover the Art of Strolling

Slowing down is an obvious way to reduce stress and prevent depression, but we can see this more easily in hindsight. How I wish that those on a fast track would heed the warning that depression can happen to anybody! Please do not simply assume that you are strong enough to cope.

Had I known that a serious loss of health through depression was in store for me, I think I would have tried almost anything to prevent it. But I did not know. I thought I was strong enough to keep up with the increasing pace of life, even though it should have been obvious that my ability to cope was decreasing. I was not strong enough. Perhaps because of the realization that I could not keep up, I fought my slower nature and moved ever more quickly to the next activity.

"You must learn to stroll instead of hurrying all the time," said my therapist friend Deana (about whom I will tell more in the next chapter, when I deal with some of the ways the Lord used to give me healing).

This sounded simple but was actually very difficult. Moving more slowly—not just mentally but physically—seemed impossible at first. People say it takes six weeks to break a bad habit and replace it with a good one. For me it took a lot longer than six weeks.

I do not mean, of course, that it is never right to run from one activity to another. Young, enthusiastic people do it often; so do older enthusiastic people, for that matter. But I was running too fast, all the time. What discipline and practice it took to stroll instead of hurry!

"Are you strolling?" Deana often asked in her checkup phone calls. Usually I was not and needed the reminder. After many weeks of practice, slower walking began to feel more normal. The simple instruction to stroll played a big part in my eventual recovery.

I became more relaxed, and as I did, I found it possible to incorporate into daily living something else that I found extremely difficult, but that Deana said was necessary to my health: breathing correctly. As I learned to focus on this, I realized that when I was tired and nervous, my breathing was quick and shallow. When I concentrated on breathing more deeply and slowly, tension melted. I could not feel tense and breathe deeply at the same time.

Lois, the friend suffering from depression whom I wrote about in chapter 4, told me that her friend Molly (herself under treatment for depression) had thanked her for the lessons on strolling, thereby promoting healing. "Don't thank me," said Lois. "I learned all I know from Pam Moore."

"Don't thank me," I told Lois, when she recounted this later. "I learned all I know from Deana."

Whom did Deana learn it from? And who will learn it from Molly? As we gain insight into factors that cause us stress, we can help others. Nonprofessionals like myself have limits on how much we can help Christians in severe depression, but surely we can do no harm if we help our stressed-out friends see bad habits in themselves that we once engaged in, too. Helping them change takes time and follow-up, but it is a way that even the least informed of us can show love and support.

Once I attended a wedding that did not seem like a wedding at all. The bride was determined to capture every moment on camera or video. She had little time to spend with the guests. I had the strange and almost surreal feeling that she was not experiencing the actual event as much as she was preserving its image for the future. Unfortunately the future was short. The marriage lasted only a few years; then her husband abandoned her and their two young daughters.

That wedding ceremony had seemed not real life but a kind of imitation. Is that what happens when we move too quickly? Is it possible that life can take on a similar surreal quality? Rather than tear through seconds, minutes and hours on fast forward, less and less able to keep pace, savor them for their immediate worth. Live in the present.

Learn to Wait

The times in which we live lead to the expectation that we can solve problems quickly. It is normal to expect swift closure, but many problems do not have immediate solutions. One example is the cancer epidemic. I do not know anybody whose personal life or that of a loved one has not been affected by this disease. There is usually no quick solution to this illness, which brings much stress to our lives. We are forced to wait. I wonder if the Lord is withholding a cure for cancer in our time so that we might learn to wait and to trust Him more.

Corrie ten Boom loved and respected her father, Casper ten Boom, very much and often quoted him. I, in turn, quote one of Father ten Boom's wise remarks to myself often: "As well as learning how to do certain things, a person must also learn how to do nothing." It reminds me that doing nothing is in itself a disciplined activity. It is to our loss if you and I are unable to do nothing. It can be done, but it takes practice.

Let's ask the Lord to teach us how to wait. As He shows us, let's encourage each other to obey Him.

Hold Plans Lightly

There has probably never been a society in which more people make more plans than America. The United States is a nation of unlimited opportunities, and its ability to carry out good plans has blessed the country and the world. American Christians can make and fulfill plans in the Lord's will with positive and far-reaching effects. But the relentless pursuit of goals can also bring overwhelming stress. Americans have high expectations. Are they sometimes too high?

I once sat with a group of students who were discussing objectives and goals and the importance of having a personal mission statement. Looking over the shoulder of one sensitive young man, I saw the underlined heading *My Sixty-Year Plan.* This amazed me. It had never occurred to me that anybody would plan that far ahead. *What if his expectations are not met?* I thought. Plans can be heavy burdens. It is best to hold plans lightly, having surrendered their fulfillment or non-fulfillment to the Lord. (A few years later that young man suffered a serious breakdown.)

I think the example of many Dutch Christians is a good one. They do not say, "I plan to do this or that," but, "If it is God's will, I. . . ." They have in mind the words of James 4:13–15:

> Now listen, you who say, "Today or tomorrow we will go to this or that city, spend a year there, carry on business and make money." Why, you do not even know what will happen tomorrow. What is your life? You are a mist that appears for

a little while and then vanishes. Instead, you ought to say, "If it is the Lord's will, we will live and do this or that."

For the Christian there is every possibility of not achieving goals that society says should be achieved. We do not have the right to success as society views it. We are not our own and do not have the right to choose our own way. We belong to the Lord. He can do anything He likes with our lives, including changing our direction in mid-course. Jumping off the success ladder in our modern-day world is a great stress-reliever.

In this chapter we have looked at seven ways to reduce some of the stress that comes from living in this difficult time. We can ask God to give us understanding of our times, remembering that He ordained that we be born in this generation. We can take definite steps to regain our lost perspective in life. We can practice the discipline of living at a deliberately slower pace and learning to wait. And we can learn to hold plans lightly. In fact, if we hold on too tightly to anything that is causing us stress, the Lord might have to pry our fingers away, and that hurts.

What Helped Me Recover from Depression

8

"I know the plans I have for you," declares the LORD, "plans to prosper you and not to harm you, plans to give you hope and a future."

Jeremiah 29:11

Even the healthiest among us often find it difficult to face the future with confidence. After all, we do not know the way. Only the Lord knows the good plans He has for us and how He will bring them about. And if the healthy person lacks confidence, how much more can the depressed person be overwhelmed with premature anticipation of tomorrow!

In my case I very much wanted a future and a hope, yet could see no way out of all-engulfing sorrow. But in spite of how I felt, the Lord restored me. I want to share with you in this chapter some of the means He used, keeping in mind that not every depressed person is restored to health exactly as I was. I cannot stress often enough that symptoms of depression differ from person to person, and that the depths of hopelessness in each case are unfathomable.

Nevertheless here are six means God used to restore me:

Medication
The Bible
Christian counseling
Prayer
Rest
Permanent changes in my way of living

All these ingredients (which are not listed in any order of importance) were vital to my healing.

Medication

Let me start with the item that, in my experience, is the most difficult for Christians to understand and agree about. The lack of understanding and agreement is not limited to Christians. Although the science of neurochemistry is rapidly acquiring new information, and we hope to have more understanding early in this third millennium, there is still much to learn about the brain. But of one thing I am sure. When at my lowest point I called to God for help, He helped me. For me medication was part of His answer. Sometimes medicine is needed at least to reach and sustain the point where the sufferer can think and reason again normally, and be able to understand the changes that need to be made in his or her life.

As I wrote earlier, although I had come to the conclusion that I was depressed, it took me nearly three weeks to pluck up the courage to make an appointment with our family doctor, an internist in the adjacent city of Arlington.

"You know what I'm going to say, don't you?" he said after I had listed my disabling systems.

"Yes," I replied.

Those symptoms sounded almost identical to the warning signs of depression about which I had read in medical and popular articles.

"You've just described some of the symptoms of clinical depression," the doctor continued. "I have many patients with the same diagnosis, and they've received the help they needed. Here's what I suggest we do for you. . . ."

He said he wanted me to try an antidepressant medication, and explained that it worked by raising the level of a chemical essential to the proper conducting of neurons in the brain. If this chemical is not present in sufficient quantity, he explained, the brain cannot function properly, and symptoms like mine are often the result. Because of my interest in things medical and the reading I had done, I knew this particular medication worked to restore the chemical called serotonin to its proper level.

The doctor talked to me for some time, and one of his prescriptions was "Get plenty of rest." That thought filled me with longing, even though at the time I could not see how it would be possible.

But so ill did I feel that late January day in 1996 that I was determined at least to try the medication the doctor had prescribed. Although I had strongly resisted the thought of taking medicine, that seemed easier to do than finding time to rest. (My failure to make time for rest was a great mistake, I was to learn later, but at the time I saw no way to do it.)

I was in for one of the biggest surprises of my life. I was amazed at how quickly the medicine worked! I began to feel very much better. The all-engulfing sadness lifted, the weepy episodes stopped and for the first time in six months I had hope.

What a vast relief it was! It was as if the real me had been restored. However was this possible? I, who had long resisted the idea of a Christian needing antidepressant medication, underwent a rapid conversion. I did not know how it worked, but when I took a small tablet each day, something happened in my brain. Because a chemical was being restored to a more correct level for normal function, I felt myself again.

But it was even more than that. It was as if something was restored that had always been missing. I became convinced that, as a child, I had had symptoms of low serotonin. A kind of assurance now came into my brain—an assurance that had not been there when, as a girl, I agonized about whether the bedroom door was shut or not shut.

In fact, I was suddenly able to do some things I had never been able to do, as far back into childhood as my memory extends. All at once, for example, I found myself able to watch American football games on television. My husband is not an avid football fan, but sometimes he likes to relax on Sunday afternoons by watching Dallas Cowboys games. I had tried to join him, but before I began to take medication, the whole of the game darted so quickly through my brain, and so erratically, that trying to follow it made me very nervous. Suddenly the reaction of my brain became more like Carey's. It was as if something in my head slowed down. I could respond to moves made by the Cowboys at the time Carey responded to them. I could watch the game and make sense of it.

It was similar with driving a car. That had always exhausted me. My brain magnified danger, as it were, anticipating it from every side, and everything seemed to move too fast for me to take it in. But driving is a pleasure now. Yes, it will always be an activity to be undertaken with great care, but my brain no longer forces me to prepare for multiple unforeseen calamities based on premature speculation about what other drivers might or might not do.

With changes like this happening, I knew I was on the road to recovery. I thanked God. I had asked Him for help, and He had answered my prayer.

Let me be quick to add two things: First, many cases of depression do not respond to medication as quickly as mine did, or at all (we will discuss this in the next chapter); and second, medicine was not all I needed.

I asked a Christian doctor friend of mine about the length of time most people stay on medication. "I always keep people on medication for four months," she told me, "even if they feel better right away. But if they don't respond at all, I may switch them to another medicine long before that. Most people need six months. If it's the second time someone has been on medication for depression, or if the person responds only slowly, I'll keep them on a year before reevaluating. The literature is pretty well established that some people do need to be on it indefinitely. These are folks who have had three or more severe bouts of depression, or who have had depression start in their youth. I wouldn't just say, 'Here's a lifetime supply,' but keep seeing them two or three times a year, and keep thinking about whether to try some time off the medication."

Now let me tell you about another vital means to my healing.

The Bible

One of the hardest things for the depressed person to convey to the well person is that it is often *impossible* to do many of the things that were quite attainable before. If you are well and have not yet gained that understanding, I implore you, on behalf of the depressed, to ask God to give you understanding.

Take concentration. We have already noted that depressed people frequently have poor concentration spans. The not-depressed person may not understand this and is all too tempted to say, "If you'd just pull yourself together, you'd be able to concentrate." Believe me, if it were possible to get out of depression by pulling ourselves together, we would all have done it long ago! Very few would fail to pull themselves together if it could be done by willpower. It cannot. Non-depressed persons must accept this fact and not make things worse by asking the impossible.

Using imagination helps here. Suppose you were rushing to finish your income tax forms by April 15 and were hit with a bad case of the flu. Suppose the fever, nausea, aches and pains made it impossible to concentrate and you missed the midnight deadline. Would you be helped or encouraged if somebody chided you for not being able to complete your tax return on time? That is a bit like the helplessness of depression—but not as bad. Even the worst cases of flu usually see recovery in a few days or weeks. Depression and its helplessness may last years. It is probably more like trying to complete your tax return with your hands and feet tightly bound, your mouth gagged and your brain like cotton wool. Depression feels a bit like that but, again, worse.

One of the most distressing impossibilities for some depressed committed Christians is that they cannot long concentrate on the truths of the Bible. I have not forgotten how our enemy, Satan, loves to distract all Christians from daily reading and meditating on the Bible, but for the clinically depressed Christian, lack of concentration is part of the illness and not wholly the work of Satan.

Since new spiritual insights can be gained in difficult times, we might expect to be helped through our trials by learning important new lessons. With depression this may or may not be the case. As I experienced losses attendant to depression (for depression is a devastating loss of health, hope and a future), I found that, rather than learning new lessons, I was helped by recalling and relearning old ones. Thus, part of my recovery from the depression diagnosed in the 1990s was remembering and reflecting on lessons learned from losses in the 1980s.

Lessons That Comforted Me

In a fairly short space of time in 1983, I lost through death my companion Corrie ten Boom, my work with her, my home in California and (as far as I knew) my new country. Most devastating of all was the loss of my dearly loved mother, who passed away at Christmas 1983, just eight months after Tante Corrie.

During 1984 I wrote down some of the ways the Lord was comforting me through His Word. These notes of lessons learned helped me greatly when I faced losses later. In fact I am using them now to share five of the ways the Word of God gave me hope during this time.

1. "SURELY GOD IS GOOD" (PSALM 73:1).

The first, never-changing fact on which to reflect is the glorious certainty of the goodness of God. What comfort and stability this brings! Let's repeat it to ourselves and to each other often. God does not count things as you and I count them. Perhaps our silent acknowledgment, in our lowest moments, that God is good is just as important to Him— and more dangerous to the accusing powers of darkness— as the most public, generous and seemingly more effective words and actions of the well Christian.

2. "MY TIMES ARE IN YOUR HANDS" (PSALM 31:15).

I often sought to call to mind during my depression this truth that I had proved many times before my depression. My times were in God's hands. That meant my circumstances were, too. Nothing I was experiencing lay outside the loving hands of God. The difficult times as well as happy times were equally in His hands.

In early 1983 God had helped me trust Him in a difficult dilemma. Corrie ten Boom, then ninety years old, was so ill that I could not leave her. Yet letters I received from England told of medical tests pointing to malignant disease in my mother. It helped me to pray, "Father, will You please so arrange things that I will always be in the right place at the right time as far as Tante Corrie and my mother are concerned?"

The Lord answered. He allowed me to assist both Corrie ten Boom and my mother in their deaths. The timing was marvelous to me. He brought me home to England after several years, exactly in time to care for my mother. Only He could have worked that out.

That memory from thirteen years before helped me know that this time of depression was in His hands, too.

3. "NOW FOR A LITTLE WHILE YOU MAY HAVE HAD TO SUFFER GRIEF IN ALL KINDS OF TRIALS" (1 PETER 1:6).

This was another truth of much comfort. My present grief and depression were not going to last forever. The pain was temporary. It was "for a little while." It would not be happening to me unless the Lord deemed it necessary. I did not know His reasons and perhaps never will completely. Whether the grief had come about through the circumstances of the times in which I am living, for my chastening and training, or for the eventual good of not just myself but others, I did not need to know.

4. "THE LORD TURNED THE CAPTIVITY OF JOB, WHEN HE PRAYED FOR HIS FRIENDS" (JOB 42:10, KJV).

The Lord is aware that it is hard for the depressed person to concentrate in prayer. Short prayers for others, sometimes simply bringing to God their names, can be enough. Praying for others not only helps put things in right perspective, but it can change our lives, as it did Job's.

5. "NAOMI RETURNED FROM MOAB ACCOMPANIED BY RUTH THE MOABITESS, HER DAUGHTER-IN-LAW, . . . AS THE BARLEY HARVEST WAS BEGINNING" (RUTH 1:22).

Here is a hope-giving truth I had learned in the past and tried to remember in my illness: You and I do not know what the Lord is planning for the time that lies beyond our present suffering.

In the first chapter of the book of Ruth, we learn that two widows, Naomi, who was Jewish, and Ruth, her daughter-in-law from Moab, traveled to Judah, Naomi's original home. Naomi had gone to Moab with her husband and two sons years before to escape famine in Judah. Then her husband and sons died and famine came to Moab. No doubt Ruth and her mother-in-law were grieving as they journeyed back to Judah. They had experienced great loss—and what could the future hold?

But the Lord was planning something very good for them. We are given a hint of it in the last verse of Ruth 1. It is easy to overlook a few words written there, but they are important: Ruth and Naomi returned "as the barley harvest was beginning." The season is significant for, as you will recall, there was to be harvesting in the fields of Boaz, a relative of Naomi. Ruth went to glean barley, found favor in the eyes of Boaz and eventually married him. Their son Obed was the grandfather of King David, into whose human lineage the Lord Jesus Christ was born.

God used the grief of death and famine to blessed purpose for Ruth, for Naomi and for the world. He is the same Lord today. Out of your present grief or depression He can bring glory. This period is significant. God, for His own reasons, may choose not to reveal the future, but His plans for His children are always good. This little verse from Ruth helped me be sure that one day I would see the beauty of His plan.

It is important that you and I read, study, learn and apply the Word of God when we are well and strong. How much harder it is to do it when we are ill and weak! So the truth and principles of the Bible must become part of us.

Letting God's Word Become Part of Us

When Corrie ten Boom lost her ability to speak, read and write in 1978 through a serious stroke, and became progressively weaker through subsequent strokes, something happened one day that I have never forgotten.

Because of brain damage, words and their meanings had been mostly lost to Tante Corrie. She might want to tell me something but could rarely find the appropriate words. One day I sat next to her bed and looked into the blue eyes of this great woman of God. I so admired her victorious stand for Christ and, at the end of her life, saw her continue to prove true many of the promises of the Bible. The fruit of the Spirit, for example, including love, joy, peace, patience, kindness, gentleness and self-control, were evident in her silent life and very weak body.

Although I never knew the level of her understanding at any point, there were times—perhaps when the oxygen supply to her brain was greater—when she could understand what I said. I came to recognize those times, and took the opportunity during one of them to ask an important question. I wanted to be sure that whatever might happen to us, we can never lose the Scripture we have committed to memory.

"Tante Corrie," I said, speaking slowly and clearly, "although you cannot now say all the Bible verses you learned, they are still in your mind, aren't they? You can hear them there, can't you?"

Tante Corrie looked sad, turned her eyes downward and shook her head.

That piece of information shocked and saddened me. She apparently no longer had the comfort of recalling the Word of God to her mind in any of the languages she knew—Dutch, English, German and French.

But then I perceived something glorious. The Word of God, which she had read, studied and applied throughout her long life, had become part of her. I tried to explain to her that I could see how the Holy Spirit, the Helper, was proving that God's Word is living and active. I could see this, and so could many others. She knew the Word and the Word knew her.

I mentioned that I have never forgotten this interchange with Tante Corrie. But since that time I do not say, "I will never *forget.*" It helps remind me that memory is a gift of God. The Lord gives, the Lord takes away. Blessed be the name of the Lord. He allowed Tante Corrie's memory for language to be taken away, and therefore, I suppose, the exact Bible wording as she had learned it in the Dutch of the nineteenth century.

Some of us, too, may face the trial of not being able to recall God's Word as we learned it. The trial could come through many causes. If it should happen to us, to our family or to our friends, will the Bible's principles and truths be so much a part of our beings that they are worked out through us to His honor, even in the silence of a stroke or the invisible anguish of depression?

Christian Counseling

Mental health professionals recommend medication with counseling as the most effective treatment for clinical depression. Although in the days before my own depression I viewed Christian counseling with suspicion, in my time of need, through the kindness of the Lord, I was to receive a special gift by the name of Deana Hancock.

A licensed professional counselor in the state of Texas, Deana had attended a singles conference in New Mexico where I spoke in 1993. She contacted me afterward, and Carey and I soon became friends with her. A single woman in her early thirties with dark hair, brown eyes and a great sense of fun, Deana accompanied and helped me on several speaking appointments. During this time she became increasingly concerned about symptoms of clinical depression that she saw in me. Knowing my aversion to psychology, and since she had to walk the line between friendship and her professional training, she waited prayerfully to approach me at the right time.

By July 1996 I had been taking my medicine for six months and was feeling much better. Carey had finished aggressive radiation and chemotherapy for his malignancy and was gaining strength. I had worked full-time as director of the university's prayer ministry for nearly eight years. Life was busier than ever, and I had to admit to deep tiredness. But I wrongly assumed that it was not so deep that I could not continue working.

Also, I was managing to keep my symptoms fairly well hidden. Dallas Baptist University is a family in which the members take care of each other and keep a lookout for those in need. As I struggled with lessening strength and ability, I reckoned that I was not the only person on campus who felt tired, so why should I bother anybody else with my problem? Besides, I had been leading the prayer ministry for eight years, reminding us all that Christians could bring things about by prayer that could not be brought about in any other way. Would it not be letting the Lord down if the director of the intercessory prayer ministry could not carry on? It might appear that prayer did not work for the one whose privilege it was to receive and disseminate thousands of prayer requests.

At least, that is what I thought. Then one day toward the end of July, I collapsed at my office. My energy was drained to the point that I was too exhausted to think or carry out any normal daily tasks. I could no longer carry on with my work. My supervisor advised me to go home, which I did immediately. I called Carey to tell him I was feeling unwell and that I had gone home. I assured him I would be all right. Then I called our friend Deana to ask for prayer.

I suppose her experience as a counselor told her that I surely was not "all right," as I had assured her and Carey. She did pray, but she also came at once to our house and found me weeping in one of the dark blue chairs in the front room.

I know that thousands of others have found themselves in that condition and thousands more will. The scene is not easy for me to recall, but I write of it hoping that my words can be used to prevent this from happening to other Christians, or to help them see how desperately the depressed Christian needs help and support.

Deana's coming that afternoon—making me tea, rubbing my feet, fetching a new box of tissues, telling me that things would one day be better, and praying with me—was the same as the Lord Jesus coming to me in acceptance, mercy and love. It is in that spirit that Christians today must serve each other and therefore serve Him. May He say to many of us on Judgment Day, "I was sick and you looked after me."

Along with checkups from my doctor, I was to have additional help. Carey and I invited Deana to suggest some specific behavioral changes that, combined with the medication, might help me.

As I look back to the time of Deana's counsel, I see clearly and thankfully that the Lord provided for me some of the best help I could have received. He is such a merciful God that in spite of my previous aversion to psychology, He sent me a good friend whose gifts of counseling helped me in my healing. Would I have sought counsel if Deana had not already been part of our lives? I do not know, but He who has plans to bless His children knows, and that is enough.

In preparation for this chapter I asked Deana if she would help me describe the kind of counseling help she gave me, so that I could pass on some of the principles. I will use some of what she wrote in response to my request. It is not meant to be a mini-course in counseling. If you are struggling with depression, perhaps this will help you see how Christian counseling might help you. If you know someone who is clinically depressed, perhaps it will help you discover a few things you might do to help, and also alert you to some attitudes and conversations that might need to be redirected.

Deana tells me that, professionally speaking, what she did for me on that day was called an *intervention*. This is a term used in the counseling profession to describe assertive action taken during a crisis. Deana had noted symptoms of depression in me, which eventually led to my becoming unable to function properly. She reminded me that she came to see me at home and at work and just let me talk about how overwhelmed

113

I was feeling. *Reflective listening* is the counseling term. She remembers my saying, "I know what you're doing, Deana. You're not saying anything so I'll talk more." And she writes:

> Of course, you were right. My responses would be reflective in that I would restate, or rather reframe, what you had already said. I believe this did two things. First, it validated how you were feeling. By this I mean that I did not refute what you told me, but rather confirmed that your feelings were sound and defensible. And second, it began the trust-building process that is essential for effective counseling, or for any healthy relationship.
>
> Reflective listening is a powerful tool in communication. It demonstrates respect. Second, without that time together before your collapse, I do not believe you would have asked for or received my help during the intervention stage. The Lord had obviously ordained that time in 1993 when we first met for the following years of mutual help and healing. Indeed, our times are in His hands.

Deana continues:

> The intervention stage was about recognizing the severity of your illness and educating your support system—Carey, family and friends. It was also an intense time of watchcare. I maintained daily contact with you. When a person is severely depressed, as you were, their thought processes are not always accurate.
>
> The *ineffective* way of dealing with inaccurate thought processes is to "correct," as in lecture, deny or minimize what is said, so I needed to be careful about the way I spoke to you. If I had said to you, "Pam, you're wrong about such and such," you would have responded in a defensive manner (as most people would). May we never underestimate our choice of words! Although I am sure I failed in this at times, I tried to offer you other ways of thinking about a situation by using lead-in words such as "Let me invite you to consider. . . ." I needed to make sure that the decision—that is, the control—

was always yours. This is important in depression because the depressed person feels out of control.

Helping you recognize normal feelings, not stay in exaggerated ones, benefited you in regaining your health. It was also essential for me to educate Carey on major depression so that he would know how to respond to you in helpful ways. For instance, answering the telephone was too stressful for you at first and had to be eliminated.

It is good to know that people care about you, but at that particular time it seemed difficult for you to handle the telephone appropriately. Even with Dorothy—you could not speak to her and your closest friends without getting upset. That was because part of depression is not hearing correctly. You could not receive your friends' attempts to help at that time. Of course, as you became better, telephone calls were a source of strength.

Deana adds:

During the intervention the basics of life were what we concentrated on—rest, exercise, eating well, taking your medicine, learning how to breathe properly, learning how to "walk" again—that is, stroll—and spending time on self-care. (I remember how you enjoyed the massage Mandy gave you.) As you became more consistently coherent, you were able to identify past and present stressors. We began to work out how one affected the other. It was neat to watch your eyes light up as you discovered something new. You began to understand some of your behaviors and figure out which adjustments worked well for you and which did not.

I remember the day Deana helped me identify something important that needed dealing with. I told her that the way ahead seemed blocked by a wall built of stones. We talked about what the stones, taken one by one, might represent. If we could identify them, perhaps they could be removed from the wall and the way ahead be made easier. We asked the Lord to help with this.

I drew a simple sketch of a wall consisting of separate bricks, and as I identified each one, I wrote its name on it. Here are some of the names:

Deep concern at the worsening health of my father in England.

Homesickness for him and for my brother and sister and their families.

A much-too-crowded speaking schedule (the engagements all accepted by me who found it hard to say no).

A private and sad situation that deeply affected the life of my family and that seemed irresolvable.

A growing sense that I could no longer carry out the job I loved as prayer ministry director at the university.

And to my surprise I began to discover that some of the stones in the wall represented people who had hurt me in the past, or situations over which I had no control that were exerting much pressure on me.

As far as I knew, I had forgiven those who had caused hurt. I did realize that I was emotionally vulnerable now and could not trust my feelings, but during that time of crisis I wanted to make sure that, as far as I was concerned, forgiveness was complete. I identified the people who had hurt me in the past, compiled a list of their names, and with the Lord's help went through the list, asking Him to help me forgive completely and to let go of any hurt I might still be feeling. I made a similar list of the stressful things that lay outside my control. As far as I knew I surrendered to the Lord the people and the circumstances.

Now I will let Deana continue recounting the ways she used counseling to help me.

Throughout the healing process I tried to tell you what might happen or what to expect. For instance, you might feel great one minute and lousy the next. Noting your progress, I tried to tell you when you were doing better and to help you anticipate what might be coming down the road. An example was when I warned you to expect setbacks, but advised you to learn to see them as times of reflection and rest, not of failure. I showed you how to track your progress by measuring the lengthening periods of time between setbacks, not just by noting the setback itself.

May I say that at the time when you were most vulnerable, I tried to be very gentle in my guidance. As you became stronger, guidance became more firm. I would not tell you what to do, but my words were more direct. In the beginning the directions were simple: "Please go to bed now." "It's time to rest." "Don't run, stroll." "Have some tea." "Let's wait on that decision or action." Later, when you were feeling better, you requested that I go with you to your office after hours to see if you could build toward the time you could return to work. I would insist you stay no longer than certain set times. "You've only got fifteen minutes." "You've got thirty minutes this time." "Take a break now."

Deana continues:

I tried to identify behaviors that showed stress, such as sighing. We worked on what the word *healthy* means for you. I asked you to make a list of what a healthy you would be like. How would you know if you had reached the point of being healthy? These are ways of setting goals and offering hope. So many times counseling keeps a person sick. I hope I have not done this. It is essential to focus on what is healthy and what healthy behaviors are. You had to learn to know what was not healthy and to discern what your body was telling you.

It goes without saying that if the Lord were not in this, you would have never recovered to the extent that you have. It is He, Jehovah Rapha, who daily offers you and me healing and help. Some of what I have said came from being a counselor, some came from personal experience and most came from the Holy Spirit and His prompting. I kept you in constant prayer—and myself, too, that I might say the right things and help you in the most appropriate ways. I prayed for hope and wisdom constantly. The most difficult part for me was letting you fly on your own. But had I not done that, it would have been harmful. It would have communicated the message that you could not do this by yourself. But fly you did!

The above words represent many hours of patient counsel and practical help to Carey and me by the Lord's counselor servant. Deana Hancock represents many in the profession of Christian counseling who work hard to assist depressed Christians in regaining their health.

Prayer

When I began work as director of the intercessory prayer ministry at Dallas Baptist University in 1988, I considered many definitions of what prayer is and what it is not. I came up with a definition that headed the list as I went about my daily work: "Prayer is not about obtaining things from God. Prayer is about knowing God. It is coming into His presence."

As I taught on prayer at the university and at meetings all over the country, I sought to balance the tension between prayer on the one hand as a gift of God, and on the other hand as a disciplined work.

During the time of my depression, it was hard to pray. I could not concentrate well, my memory was impaired and I was thoroughly weary. It was hard to do any work, and prayer is work. I do not mean that I did not pray, but I certainly prayed less. I am not recommending that Christians should pray less, but I want to underline that the Lord, who knew my weakness, was very merciful. Just coming to Him sometimes was enough. Placing my jumbled thoughts before Him, without particular word structure or specific request, was sufficient.

Having said that, however, I must add that offering up sufficient prayer is vital, even if the depressed Christian does not do the praying herself. When I became ill I sent messages to my family, friends and prayer partners asking for prayer. Prayer is a gift of God, a vital weapon of our warfare. Without it we cannot become all that the Lord wants us to be. I discovered that when I could not pray much because of depression, others did it for me. I kept and treasure many of the letters I received assuring me of prayer.

As I have said, things can be brought about by prayer that cannot be brought about in any other way. Prayer was an indispensable part of my healing.

Rest

Soon after I became unable to work and had to leave my office, my supervisor came to visit me at home. She brought the news that the university administration was granting me a leave of absence for the coming five months. They would not expect me to return to my office until the beginning of January 1997.

Such a possibility had not occurred to me. Because I realized the seriousness of my condition and that recovery would take time, I accepted the leave of absence with relief and much gratitude.

Learning to rest (an ongoing process indeed!) was much more than not being at my daily work for a certain amount of time each day. I had to learn to slow down. Learning to rest meant deliberate, difficult changes. Instead of scurrying everywhere, I had to learn to walk. I had to learn to say no to invitations when accepting them would have taken more strength than I had.

Learning to rest was, and is, humbling. I still like to think that I can take on every challenge that comes my way, but I am learning that the Lord is not asking me to do that. No one person can ever meet the needs around him or her. The need is not the call. Our call is to come to Jesus Christ and receive rest; and from that rest we respond as the Holy Spirit prompts us. Without it we cannot respond aright, for the Spirit speaks softly.

Learning to rest means obeying the Holy Spirit's prompt-ings to move out of whatever we might be involved in—to walk in the fresh air, to view the stars, to take a nap, to read poetry, to do whatever it is that our beings, made in the image of God, need in order to live life abundantly.

Permanent Changes in My Way of Living

The last of the six things of particular help in my recovery is a result of the other five—the Word of God, prayer, med-icine, counsel and rest. Carey and I came to realize that some big changes needed to be made if we were to simplify our lives and cut down on stress. We prayed together and asked God to show us His will.

In the last chapter I described our move from a house in the busy city to a much quieter one in the country. Another big change, and a difficult one for me to make, was to request that I no longer work full-time at the university but move into a part-time position. This was kindly granted me.

I am learning to live differently, with less urgency, to breathe more deeply, to walk the country roads more often, to leave until tomorrow jobs I would like to complete today. And—quite a momentous change!—Annabelle entered our life.

In the autumn of 1996, during my time of crisis away from the office, Carey and I went to a farmhouse north of Dallas and bought a standard poodle. It had taken a while for me to persuade Carey (who did not want a small, fancy dog) that standard poodles are large and that we did not have to have her groomed in a fancy way. Then we found an advertise-ment in the *Dallas Morning News* for a six-month-old black puppy. The asking price was lower than for other standard poodles, and we learned that she was being sold at a discount because of an accident that had caused a broken pelvis when she was very small. She looked healthy to us and we bought her and took her home.

I named her Annabelle after a restaurant in a city in the Deep South where I had spoken recently. She was a Southern dog, I reckoned, ladylike and charming. I had never had a dog before and knew little about them. But I had heard a sermon once in which a faithful dog was compared to the servant girl in Psalm 123:2: "As the eyes of a maid look to the hand of her mistress, so our eyes look to the LORD our God." It would be nice to train Annabelle, I thought, to give the same deference to her owners as the maidservant gave her mistress. I could use our poodle in my talks as an example of trustful obedience.

This proved harder than I thought! For one thing Annabelle often did not act in a ladylike way, was not always charming and, although clearly intelligent, did not appear to understand the word *no*. We decided the best thing would be to take her to a local dog-training kennel as a boarder for ten days. (Deana's reaction was to laugh and liken the obedience training sessions to human therapy!)

Annabelle received individual therapy (learning to obey commands from her trainer), family therapy (sessions with her trainer and with us) and group therapy (with her trainer and other dogs.) She came home a different dog. We learned how to reinforce the lessons she had learned, and now cannot imagine life without her. She races like a greyhound, prances and bounces, runs in circles, defends us passionately, cocks her elegant head quizzically, licks us and loves us quite unconditionally.

While she will probably never be the picture of perfect obedience shown in Psalm 123, in which the maidservant watches her mistress constantly, Annabelle obeys us most of the time and has brought much fun and joy into our lives. From the beginning I laughed at her antics in a way I had not heard myself laugh in many years. I confess we are rather besotted with our dog. We take her for walks, play with her and mock fight with her.

Dogs require a great deal of attention, and getting one is a decision to be made not lightly but with prayer and great care. But, amazingly, the need to take care of Annabelle has brought rest into our lives. For instance, we do not stay away from home and leave her alone for more than a certain number of hours. I am more relaxed because of Annabelle, and stronger. In fact, I am better able to take care of my husband and my part of the household responsibilities and to do my daily work.

So Carey and I have made some important changes: We moved to the quiet countryside, I began to work part-time, a dog joined our household. We have made other changes, too, the implementation of which has taken time, and the Lord has blessed them.

The Bible, rest, medicine, prayer, counsel, changes in our way of living—these are six important ways the Lord brought and is maintaining healing in my life. For you, or for those you love who are depressed, all these things, or perhaps some of them, may be part of healing.

You might say, "Well, I'm glad for you, but the kind of help you received couldn't happen to me." In the coming two chapters I want to show that this kind of help can indeed happen to you or to those you love, and to discuss how it can be brought about.

What Can a Depressed Christian Do?

9

Heal me, O Lᴏʀᴅ, and I will be healed;
save me and I will be saved, for you are
the one I praise.

Jeremiah 17:14

In this chapter we will explore
some ways Christians can help themselves
through depression. I begin it with the
hope and prayer that my words will not
come across to depressed Christians as
trite, or holding any hint that if only he or
she would heed this or that advice, everything would be all right. Those who are
depressed may find it impossible to order
their thoughts, to remember what they
have read or to take any initiative. In addition, the pointers in this chapter may not
apply to every case. And some of these suggestions will already have been acted on by
many.

We have noted that depression is a serious disease requiring serious, professional
treatment. Successful treatment is possi-

ble in most cases, but many depressed Christians do not seek help. How can we change this?

Accept the Fact That You Are Depressed

In the first chapter I described my own struggle in accepting the fact that I was depressed and that depression was an illness. But the day came when I had to admit it, and from then on I began to take steps on the highway to recovery.

One of the reasons many of us find it hard to admit we have clinical depression is the fact that it is a mental illness. Just the other morning I glanced through the *Dallas Morning News* and came across these words from Cynthia Hammer, president of the National Alliance for the Mentally Ill in Pierce County, Washington: "Depression—along with a whole host of other neurobiological brain disorders—*is* a mental illness." This is tough for many to hear.

But accepting depression as mental illness (the term *brain disorder* is now preferred by mental health professionals) does not require defeated resignation. It means taking an active stance. For Christians acceptance is the honest and heartfelt acknowledgment (as far as our depressed condition permits anything to be heartfelt!) that we have a brain disorder. And that our sovereign God has allowed this difficult thing for purposes that only He knows. He will eventually use our suffering for good.

This acceptance is vital to healing.

Ask God for Help

Accepting our depressed condition does not mean we stop doing all we can to find a cure. First we must ask God for help. As I wrote earlier, if you cannot concentrate long enough for what might be called a proper prayer, just say, "Lord, please help me." "Help!" is enough if that is all you can do.

The Lord knows the depressed Christian needs help, but it is still important to ask Him for it. You may not feel any faith, but the fact that you have asked Him for help may be a bigger step of faith in His eyes than an apparently huge faith venture by a Christian who is strong and well.

One day in the Temple Jesus watched a crowd of people depositing money into the treasury receptacle. He saw the wealthy throw in large amounts.

> But a poor widow came and put in two very small copper coins, worth only a fraction of a penny. Calling his disciples to him, Jesus said, "I tell you the truth, this poor widow has put more into the treasury than all the others. They all gave out of their wealth; but she, out of her poverty, put in everything—all she had to live on."
>
> Mark 12:42–44

Although this gospel account refers to money, the principle goes deeper: It pleases the Lord when we give Him all we have. The widow showed great faith. She gave out of her poverty. She had nothing but those two very small copper coins to live on. Sometimes clinical depression means that a person cannot give out of her wealth. She wishes that her faith and prayers could be admirably large; they are not. But the fact that she comes at all pleases the Lord. Regardless of our feelings, those who apply to Him will never be turned away. If "Lord, help!" is all we can pray, the Lord will hear and answer.

In *The Screwtape Letters* C. S. Lewis wrote:

> The worse one is praying, the longer one's prayers take. . . . I have a notion that what seem our worst prayers may really be, in God's eyes, our best. Those, I mean, which are least supported by devotional feeling and contend with the greatest disinclination. For these, perhaps, being nearly all will, come from a deeper level than feeling. In feeling there is so much that is not really ours—so much that comes from

weather and health or from the last book read. One thing seems certain. It is no good angling for the rich moments. God sometimes seems to speak to us most intimately when He catches us, as it were, off our guard. Our preparations to receive Him sometimes have the opposite effect.

The important thing is not the wording but the heart's desire and intent. It is not wrong to be unable to find words with which to pray when we are ill with depression. But it is wrong not to want to pray at all. If we ask God for help with all our hearts, with all the sincere intent we can offer Him, He will certainly answer us.

Ask God for the Gift of Faith to Know He Has a Plan for Your Recovery

During my recovery I was overjoyed with my returning health, and thanked God for what He was doing. About this same time I started to be concerned that Gwen, a colleague and friend who was suffering from severe depression after the death of her father, might not be receiving the help toward recovery that she needed. It was a groundless concern because Gwen had asked God for help, too, and was receiving from Him exactly what she needed. She told me about it in a letter:

I want you to hear some specifics of how my life has improved. To start with, the medicine the doctor prescribed for me really kicked in about a week ago. I cannot believe the difference, and several people, including two students, have commented on how different I am than when classes began. The day looks bright, the exhaustion is gone, I *want* to get up in the morning, and I *want* to work. The Lord is so good in providing medical doctors who discovered drugs that can help us through the tough times. My roommate is thanking God, too, after having to put up with me for so long in the state I was in.

Another important thing is that I have found a Christian grief support group just three miles from my house. It is held on Monday evenings from seven to nine P.M. and is to last for six weeks. So far I have been greatly encouraged by sharing my own distress with the group and hearing about the things that have helped them. Together we are finding our way through this sad part of our lives. The group facilitator guides our sessions. This week we discussed journal-keeping and how it can be a form of prayer. It also can help us track our progress by seeing where we have been, where we are and where we are heading in our walk with the Lord. We open and close the grief meetings in prayer! Can you believe the Lord gave me this group?

Gwen, who is never happier than when she is giving to others, went on to tell the following:

On the phone a month before the group began, the facilitator, Harriett, whom I had not met, told me there was a ten dollar fee, but that it could be waived for anyone who could not afford it. The Lord put on my heart last Monday to write my check for twenty dollars in case there was someone who couldn't pay. I told Harriett this when I met her and gave her my check. Five minutes later a person came in who didn't know about the charge, and when Harriett told her, the woman said, "Oh, I just can't afford it." Harriett said, "It's no problem at all. Someone just paid twenty dollars in case another person couldn't pay." Neat, huh?

When I read this, I knew Gwen was doing better! This is part of a longer letter in which she told of many ways God was answering her prayer for help. God will answer your prayer for help, too.

Seek Medical Advice

Please make a doctor's appointment and keep it. A good place to start is your family doctor.

I wish I did not have to make the next point. Since clinical depression affects nearly twice as many women as men, it is important that a woman makes sure that the doctor she consults, if he is a male, respects and listens to women. Although it is less common today for doctors to treat women as if their depressed state were their own fault and to fail to take them seriously, it still happens too frequently. I have talked to a number of women who know they need the help of a physician but are afraid of the response they might be given by their family doctors. And, fearing the same might be true of other doctors they consult, they put off making an appointment.

Please do not delay. If your doctor is a woman, I hope that you need not fear patronizing remarks. And there are many understanding male doctors. Pray to be led to the right one, and make an appointment to see if medical help is needed in your case.

Another point: The body's declining production of the hormone estrogen before and during menopause has brought on depression in many women. My friend Elaine, a mature and wise Christian, says she turned into a different person at menopause, thoroughly alarming her husband. She felt and expressed anger in a way that frightened her, too, because sometimes it seemed impossible to control. Although it is hard for me to imagine, she tells of throwing things across the living room and, on one occasion, only just refraining from emptying a bucket of white paint on her husband during a mild disagreement! Elaine visited her doctor, who prescribed hormone replacement therapy (HRT). In a short time Elaine was her old self.

Every woman needs to decide, in consultation with her doctor, whether HRT is right for her.

Accept the Fact That You May Need an Antidepressant

The change in my health after a short time of taking an antidepressant was, as I have mentioned, one of the most remarkable things I have ever experienced. Antidepressants are a group of medicines that work specifically on brain chemistry. There had been an imbalance in some of my brain chemicals called neurotransmitters. A neurotransmitter is a chemical messenger found in the brain and wherever there are nerves. It takes messages from one neuron (nerve) to another. Neurotransmitters (nerve transmitters) keep the neurons in the brain talking to each other. Without proper balance, the conducting of messages from one brain cell to another cannot take place efficiently.

Some Christians have told me that their cases of clinical depression have not responded to antidepressant medicine. After several attempts to find a medication that worked, they abandoned the search, as well as the hope that medicine could ever help them. Others have told me that after a long search, the right antidepressant was found and healing came. Neurochemical research is yielding more and more of depression's secrets, and it could be that medical help will soon be available for those who, up until now, have not found relief.

Don't give up. Do keep yourself as informed as possible about pharmacological advances. Please persevere.

At the same time it is important to remember that antidepressants should never be viewed as the whole answer. My doctor friend, Jennifer, says, "I'd say that medication may be one part of the answer, and should be discussed with your doctor as a possibility. The trouble here is that so many doctors are more than willing to fling pills at someone just to get them out of their offices. It's easier to write a prescription than to talk about what the root causes of the problem are. There are time pressures, too, especially in today's 'managed care' world. How can I explore in a ten-minute time slot whether a patient is really bitter toward her mother? Medication helps a lot of the time, but when a patient is depressed because he or she is deeply angry at someone, or hasn't forgiven, or doesn't want to acknowledge some hard life experience, medicine does not help much."

129

Seek Other Avenues to Healing

In the previous chapter I told of six areas in which I pursued help in my recovery from depression. Because for me each of these areas was vital, I urge you to get help in searching out the important components that will be part of your own healing. Medicine is often very helpful, but it is never the only answer.

As for me, I believe my kind of depression can run in families. Often I remind myself of my paternal grandmother, who had symptoms of depression. But I am not a genetic robot. None of us is. A tendency toward depression does not give you or me freedom from responsibilities. Nor does it give us an excuse to do less than our best in finding and following through on treatment and accompanying changes in behavior where necessary.

An example of changing behaviors for me was to recognize and admit that I was working too hard. I had to change that. It was difficult because hard work was a deeply ingrained habit. I love the feeling of accomplishment at a challenge completed. I must also admit that I like to appear productively occupied all the time! But a change had to come. I now take up fewer challenges. I have learned to say, "I wish I could, but I am unable to at this time," when fitting in another appointment would take so much energy that existing appointments would suffer. I work less hard now. Once or twice the thought has stolen across my mind that with fewer busywork activities, I might actually be getting more important things done. Is this because a slower approach to work gives opportunity for better planning? Or simply because I am far less concerned about the outcome of my work than I used to be? This altered perspective can also be learned.

Be Open about Your Depression

On the night He was betrayed, the Lord Jesus walked with His disciples to the Garden of Gethsemane. If anybody knew sorrow, it was He. The Lord was honest about His anguish, admitting it to Himself and the disciples: "My soul is overwhelmed with sorrow to the point of death" (Matthew 26:38). He was honest with God: "My Father, if it is possible, may this cup be taken from me. Yet not as I will, but as you will" (verse 39). He brought the disciples in on His need: "Stay here and keep watch with me" (verse 38).

Attempting to hide depression can waste your already small supply of energy that could be used in more constructive ways. I do not mean you should broadcast your illness in an exaggerated way, but please do not isolate yourself. There is nothing to be ashamed of. Your willingness to be open could help many other depressed Christians identify with you and step out of their own isolation.

Dr. Philip G. Zimbardo from Stanford University wrote in "The Age of Indifference" (*Psychology Today*, August 1980):

> I know of no more potent killer than isolation. There is no more destructive influence on physical and mental health than the isolation of you from me and us from them. It has been shown to be a central agent in the etiology of depression, paranoia, schizophrenia, rape, suicide, mass murder, and a wide variety of disease states.

There is a profound reason we should not keep our depression secret, however vulnerable we must become in order to do it. This reason has to do with the question of suffering. Although nobody has ever come up with a satisfactory explanation from the human point of view for suffering, sometimes God gives us glimpses into the mystery.

From our viewpoint we might realize that love is always predicated on someone else's need. Were there no sinners, there would be no need of a Redeemer. Were there no pain, there would be no need for somebody to assuage that pain; no hunger, no need for anybody to supply food; no loneliness, no need for a companion; no weakness, no need for the strong to help the weak. There must be objects in need before the community of faith can meet those needs. Those who give love to the needy by meeting their needs receive great blessing and a deep sense of fulfilling the purpose for which they were created. This is because it is God's own love that is being extended.

I know that a good part of the reason I received so much help during my time of deep depression is simply that I sought it. I was extremely open about my need.

When we, the depressed, are willing to be vulnerable and allow others to see our needs, wonderful things happen! Not only will we be helped through their supply of our needs, but we can become the opportunity for others to experience growth. May the Lord help us be willing to let our hurt show so that others may grow in love. In this way we volunteer ourselves to give people the opportunity for God's nature of goodness and love to be made more fully known.

Eat Well

Some depression sufferers do not eat enough; others tend to overeat. It is important to eat well-balanced meals and avoid extremes. Ask a friend to help you with this. Discuss your diet with her or him and ask for assistance in seeing that you eat healthy food regularly. Perhaps you are not well enough to concentrate on such reading at the moment, but when the time comes, please inform yourself of the role of nutrition in healthy emotional responses. (One such book, *How to Heal Depression* by Harold Bloomfield and Peter McWilliams, has a section on healthy eating and is listed in "Recommended Reading.")

Exercise

For most of us it takes extraordinary effort to maintain this discipline. I need the help of a membership at the YMCA and the kinesiology department's wellness program at the university. This kind of accountability helps me greatly.

Enlist the help of a friend if such accountability is the best way for you to keep up regular exercise. Exercise helps in many ways, including the improvement of sleeping and eating patterns. It also causes endorphins to be released in the brain. These act as mood elevators.

Use the Gift of Music

King George I of England suffered from depression and asked his advisers to find a musician who could help soothe his troubled mind. George Frederick Handel was presented with that challenge. The orchestral *Water Music* (1717) was one result.

A friend who has known severe depression told me she sought to fill her home with Christian praise music. "By using mental resolve I was unable to do anything about my tormented feelings," she told me. "But my spirit responded to the music, and it lifted me up."

Always Forgive

When the Lord Jesus tells us to forgive our enemies, He gives us the power that this requires. It can seem impossible to forgive a person, or several people, who have treated us badly, but anger and bitterness, especially when prolonged, can have a part in causing depression and delaying its healing. The anger so prevalent in depression is usually the result of having been hurt. It is important that we discover the reason for our anger, if it is present.

The scriptural practice of forgiveness is usually taught as the Christian's duty toward the offender, but it can also—and perhaps first—bring emotional and even physical healing to the one who does the forgiving.

"You are never so free as when you forgive your enemies," proclaimed Corrie ten Boom to audiences all over the world.

One of the first things she told me when I joined her as companion in 1976 was that, at 83 years of age, she tended to be forgetful. "When I prepare my talks," she said, "don't let me forget to have in my notes the word *forgiveness* to remind me to teach the people about it every time I speak."

This is the story she would tell.

One day at the end of the 1940s, she spoke in a church in Munich, Germany. As she looked out at individual faces in the audience, she saw a man who would not look into her eyes. Then she recognized him. The man had been a guard at Ravensbrück concentration camp where Corrie and her sister, Betsie, had been incarcerated in 1944. He had been cruel to Betsie as she was dying. Why had the guard come to the meeting?

At the end of Tante Corrie's talk, people lined up to meet her, including the guard. When his turn came, he held out his hand and said, "Fräulein, I read in the newspaper that you were to speak here. You may not remember me, but I was a guard at Ravensbrück. Since that time I have become a Christian, and I have asked God for the miracle that I may ask forgiveness of one of my former victims. That is why I came to this meeting. Fräulein, will you forgive me?"

Tante Corrie held her hand tightly behind her back. She could not shake the outstretched hand. All she could think of was Betsie's suffering at that hand. But she knew from Matthew 6 that if we do not forgive our enemies, neither shall we receive forgiveness from the Father. She then made a quick prayer: *Lord, help me.*

At that moment there came into her mind the words from Romans 5:5, which she always quoted in the King James Version: "The love of God is shed abroad in our hearts by the Holy Ghost which is given unto us."

Through these words she was helped to see that, although it was impossible for her to summon up love and forgiveness for the guard, if she allowed the Holy Spirit to do it through her, it was possible.

And she did allow Him to. She took her hand from behind her back and clasped that of the guard, saying, "Brother, I forgive you."

For more than three decades after that, Corrie ten Boom traveled the world teaching people how to forgive. Her act of forgiveness benefited the guard, but it liberated her even more. And it resulted in countless other people's learning to forgive.

Please ask the Lord to show you if there are any people against whom you hold grudges. Ask Him to help you forgive. Sometimes this means visiting, telephoning or writing the individual, expressing forgiveness for the hurt against you. (In some cases the offender has no idea that he has hurt somebody.) Contacting the person is not always necessary and is sometimes not advisable. Go through the process very deliberately with the Lord. He will help you know what to do. As the cover story of the January 10, 2000, issue of *Christianity Today* well illustrates, social scientists are discovering that "forgiveness may lead to victims' emotional and even physical healing and wholeness."

In the next chapter we will look at ways that those in the Church who are well can help those who are depressed. I hope that if you are depressed, you will be shown ways to make your needs known to those who are uninitiated about this illness, but who would find joy serving the Lord by looking after you and others. And if you are well, I hope you will learn how to involve those who, at present, do not care much about the subject of depression, but who could learn to care. We must all remember, depression can happen to anybody.

As those who are well in the Church and those who are depressed move toward each other, the Lord will be pleased with His servants. And the world will see how Christians love one another.

Helping
Depressed
Christians

Carry each other's burdens, and in this
way you will fulfill the law of Christ.

Galatians 6:2

For years suicide was the second-
leading cause of death (after accidental
injuries) among the 350,000 personnel of
the United States Air Force. Then in 1995
that branch of the military introduced a Suicide Prevention Program aimed at reducing
members' resistance to seeing a counselor
and talking about personal problems.
According to a late 1999 report of the Cen-
ters for Disease Control and Prevention, the
Air Force's Suicide Prevention Program has
helped reduce suicides by fully fifty percent.
The numbers dropped from 68 suicides in
1994 to 34 in 1998. In the first eight months
of 1999, there were only eight.

It cannot be stated too frequently that
depression plays a large part in most suicides. Nor can it be overemphasized that
the incidence of depression is rising, and

that it looks as if completed suicides will rise proportionately. But may we not conclude, at the very least, from the example of the U.S. Air Force, that encouraging people to reach out for help without fear of ridicule or rejection can significantly reduce the suicide rate?

Because suicide attempts succeed in one out of ten cases, researchers estimate that depression will be the number-two killer (outranked only by heart disease) by the year 2020. Those of us who are well—both those who have not experienced major depression and those who have—must help. Believers still recovering from depression can be of special help, I think, not just to the depressed but to those seeking to understand the depressed. This is an important part of our ministry to the Lord Jesus, before whom we will one day stand.

It is encouraging from the Air Force report that suicide rates among men and women encouraged to see a therapist and talk out their problems fell sharply. You and I may not be professional therapists, but anything we can do to show love, give hope and seek understanding can break down resistance the depressed Christian may feel about seeking help. Many do need the help of a professional Christian counselor, and our efforts can help them get it.

A chaplain friend of Carey's and mine, Sam, who lives in Dallas, volunteered to talk to me about his experience with depression. His main symptom, as he described it, was "sleepiness." He found it hard to get up mornings, and during lulls in his daily work he sometimes found himself as if in a stupor at his desk. Sam decided something was seriously wrong when he drifted off to sleep at a stoplight during his drive to work one morning. After consulting a doctor, he was diagnosed with clinical depression and began to take medication.

He and his wife have a strong marriage, but Sam says that Jane was in denial for a long time. At first she thought he had a spiritual problem that needed a spiritual solution. As a chaplain Sam understood that response; he told me he has seen it in his work many times. The message the Christian Church sometimes gives is that a depressed person is being weak and needs to get over it. How can we let this attitude persist? The Church ought to be the safest place for the Christian!—a place where weakness can be admitted. When people do not feel safe from being misunderstood, they tend to keep the problem of depression to themselves. But depression loses much of its power when it is exposed.

Sam and I also talked about the strongly independent nature of Americans, which makes vulnerability hard to admit. In a culture that lauds strength, depression is seen as a sign of weakness. The depressed American Christian feels that he fails both of his cultures, then—the American one and the Church one. The work ethic adds further guilt. Pressure is often put on people to be highly productive, but depressed people find it hard to be productive. They are, therefore, further regarded as weak. Colleagues and co-workers display little patience with a person ill with depression.

Sam admitted to me that his work was a major component in his depression. "Work was my identity," he explained. "I didn't want to face the fact that my work was a big reason for my depression because I did not want to retire from it. I now know I should have stepped out earlier."

Hindrances in Giving Help

What are some of the hindrances that well Christians experience about taking care of depressed fellow Christians?

- Some believe (as we have said) that depression is not an illness and that sadness or isolation is caused by sin or lack of trust in God: "The sad person needs to get right with God and then snap out of it!" This view is not as common as it was, but it still exists.

138

- Some people are afraid of doing more harm than good: "I don't know much about depression. A little knowledge is a dangerous thing. I might even do the person harm. I've heard that helping the depressed is best left to the professionals."
- Others are afraid that helping a depressed friend or acquaintance will turn into an ongoing commitment: "What if this person begins to rely on me for help? I couldn't handle it. There are too many people in my family and church who rely on me already."
- Some do not want negative repercussions: "I need more times of fun and laughter to bring balance to my already overstressed life. It is unlikely I will have fun with a depressed person. Plus it makes me uncomfortable."
- Some simply don't know where to begin: "I have no example to follow. I don't know anybody, apart from professionals, who actively helps the depressed."

In spite of these objections, we must ask God to show us our part in helping a depressed friend. Do well Christians seeking to minister to the depressed have the courage:

- To accept this illness as often a chemical imbalance?
- To accept medical intervention when necessary?
- To admit that depression is
    No respecter of persons?
    Not always about faithlessness?
    The number-one killer of the elderly, the number-two killer of teens?
    Not always about lack of prayer?
    Not always about demonic interference?
- To become adequately informed?
- To learn to minister more effectively?

Ministering to the Depressed

Before moving to positive ways to help, may I first list some things not to do?

- Please do not give advice. Do not say, "If only you would . . ." or, "You should. . . ."
- Please do not give sympathy.
- Please do not attempt to control or usurp control of the depressed.
- Please do not give unlimited financial help.
- Please do not be patronizing.
- Please do not reason, especially spiritually.

Dorothy Shellenberger, my "American mother," who tells her powerful story about depression in Appendix C on page 195, says that worse than all other admonitions was the one she heard over and over again in more or less the same words: "What do you have to be depressed about? You have a loving husband, four healthy children, a beautiful home. . . ."

Avoid telling the depressed person that your Uncle Rupert had the same symptoms and describing how he was or was not helped. This does not help the depressed person. It is hard for him to concentrate anyway, and he will be made more tired and even irritated by Uncle Rupert's story. He will also think you are not listening to him. Remember that a depressed person often does not "hear" things correctly. Depression makes a person self-centered and self-absorbed. The self-centeredness of depression can be one of the greatest griefs of the sufferer.

"Oh, I despise the selfishness of depression," said a strong yet depressed Christian to me in a telephone conversation between Dallas and East Texas one day. "It is totally self-absorbing. If only people understood that no amount of willpower can break the self-centeredness of it."

Christians must become the first and not the last (as is unfortunately often the case) to help break down the cruel prejudices against the depressed and those with other mental illnesses.

Mike Ashworth, Ph.D., is currently the director of psychology services for Green Oaks Behavioral Healthcare Services in Dallas. Previously he served as the program manager of the Green Oaks rehabilitation program for adults who have a severe and persistent mental illness. He asked that group of patients to provide suggestions on how to treat a person with a mental illness.

1. Don't be afraid of us. Despite what you see on TV and in the movies, studies show that the mentally ill population does not have a greater propensity toward violence than anyone else.
2. Please avoid negative stereotypical words such as *psycho, nuts, schizo, loonies*, etc. The emotional pain these dehumanizing words inflict on us hurts worse than our illness does.
3. Give us a job opportunity. Abraham Lincoln and Winston Churchill, both of whom experienced mental illness, held two of the most important jobs in history. Many of us are intelligent and long for the chance to be productive members of society.
4. Please don't tell us that if we just tried harder we could "snap out of it." This insults our intelligence and implies that we are lazy. There is nothing fun or positive about having a mental illness and none of us chooses to have it.
5. Be patient when you notice we are having a difficult time. It is O.K. to ask us if we need help.
6. Don't ask if we have taken our medication when we are angry, sad or irritable. These questions make us feel as if we don't have the right to experience normal

141

human emotions without being viewed as having an "episode."

7. Treat us as you would anyone else. We have a need for acceptance, just as you do. Most of us lead quite normal lives complete with families, children, employment and financial responsibilities.

Three of the gospels (Matthew 9:2, Mark 2:3–5 and Luke 5:18–20) describe a paralyzed man who was brought by his friends to the Lord Jesus and received healing. It is helpful to meditate on the above Scriptures and place ourselves, as ministers to the depressed of our day, in the position of the friends of that sick man of the first century.

We can also use our imaginations to add some other positive ways we might be able to help. Imagination is one of God's greatest gifts. He can use a surrendered imagination in immeasurable ways. Let's use our imaginations to gain an idea of how the depressed might be suffering. Most of us know what it is like to be depressed in some form because we have known major losses. If you have not known depression deeply, ask God to help you apply your gift of imagination to see how another may be suffering, even to the point that he or she has absolutely no hope. (The fact is, of course, there *is* hope. But we must learn to identify with the depressed, for whom reality seems far different.)

As his friends did for the paralyzed man of the gospels, so can we do for the depressed. We can exercise:

A Ministry of Presence

The depressed person often has an unreasonable fear of being abandoned. She needs assurance that this fear will not turn into reality. Tell her you want to be there for her and that she will not lose your love and support.

A Ministry of Listening

The depressed are often self-deprecating and full of complaints. We must learn to listen actively in order to respond in a way that does not contradict our friend. Otherwise he will think we do not understand, and feel further isolated.

He may say, for example, "Nothing is ever going to get any better. Life is simply not worth living."

Don't say: "Of course things will get better. Every cloud has a silver lining. And just look at all the things that make life worth living for you."

Do say: "I know it feels like that just now. But you're going to get through this, and I want to help you get through it."

A Ministry of Empathy

My dictionary tells me that empathy is the power of projecting one's personality into (and so fully comprehending) the object of contemplation. With the Lord's help we can learn how to do this.

Sympathy is not helpful. To have sympathy is to be simultaneously affected by the same feeling that the other has. It can foster self-pity and sap energy. Empathy means having the mind of an observer, detaching ourselves in order to respond to the feelings that are behind the depressed person's statements, rather than to the literal content of the statements.

In chapter 2 we talked about the invisible pain of depression. How can the Christian world be sensitive to hurting, depressed people when their pain is invisible? My Christian doctor friend, Jennifer, helped me understand an aspect of this. "When I'm asking people about their medical problems," she explained, "and as they respond, I sense myself feeling sadder and sadder, I have trained myself to ask a question: Is this person depressed? This is a fancy psychiatric concept called *countertransference*. I start feeling the person's inner pain. This takes sensitivity, and although it

143

Finding Your Way through Depression

is perhaps not realistic for the average church relationship, it is certainly applicable for someone very close to the suffering person."

A Ministry of Information

Ask your pastor what resources your church has for dealing with the depressed. Offer to help provide more resources (including those of the community) if they are needed. Does the church have the names of trained professionals to whom members can turn for counsel? Which books are available in the church library concerning depression?

A Ministry of Hope

Because hopelessness is a frequent companion to the depressed, reassure her that this is a symptom of her illness and is not reality. Tell her she will get better but that it will take time. Others have regained hope and so can she.

When I was ill as a girl with pneumonia, and later appendicitis, my mother gave me hope as she waited in the hospital with me: "You will not always feel this bad. You're going to get better." I use her words often when I want to give hope to those in pain.

A Ministry of Faith

Faith is not mental or spiritual assent. It is essentially active. The four men who took their paralyzed friend to Jesus introduced him to the Lord in a way that had probably not been done before. They climbed onto the roof of the house where Jesus was teaching, poked a hole through the roof and lowered their friend down on ropes to Jesus' feet. He received healing. God inspired them with the faith to reach the Savior in that unusual way.

144

Let's ask God for a gift of faith concerning the depressed friend we want to help. He will show us the steps that need to be taken for that friend to receive healing.

A Ministry of Looking After

When I was going through the most difficult stage of depression, I was looked after kindly not only by my husband but also by my therapist friend Deana. She was very thoughtful and generous in her care, making countless cups of tea, playing videos of *I Love Lucy* and, on more than one occasion, helping me sort out piles of paperwork in my neglected study at home. This was a relief to me and a great help in my taking steps forward, small though they often were.

A Ministry of Prayer

Ongoing prayer for, and possibly with, our depressed friends is vital. It is right to pray for certain things, and we must. God likes specific prayer. Definite prayers receive definite answers.

There is one aspect to prayer that we neglect to our peril—that of praying not just *for* things, but *against* things, particularly against Satan. As we discussed in chapter 6, it is Satan's plan to steal, kill and destroy.

When the disciples asked Jesus to teach them to pray, one of the things He told them to ask was, "Deliver us from the evil one" (Matthew 6:13). Asking the Father to keep us from Satan's power is just as important as "Give us today our daily bread." And in His high priestly prayer, the Lord Jesus besought the Father on our behalf, "My prayer is not that you take them out of the world but that you protect them from the evil one" (John 17:15).

In our prayers, petitions and intercessions, we must specifically ask the Father to keep us and all His children from the evil one. This is very important. The Lord Jesus told us to do it. And we must certainly be careful to pray this for the depressed, whom Satan delights in discouraging.

A Ministry of Accountability

As we involve ourselves in the lives of a depressed person, a team of two develops. It is important to discuss goals and to note progress.

One of my difficulties in depression was the inability to concentrate on one task at a time. I was easily distracted and sometimes found it almost impossible to follow through. In her patient and non-pushy way, Deana helped me learn to focus and to undertake one task at a time (something I am still learning!). Careful not to exert pressure, she held me accountable by asking how things were coming on matters we had discussed. This gave me increased impetus to do better.

The Depressed and Bible Study

"The word of God is living and active. Sharper than any double-edged sword, it penetrates even to dividing soul and spirit, joints and marrow; it judges the thoughts and attitudes of the heart" (Hebrews 4:12).

It also penetrates depression, psychosis, mental illness and spiritual oppression. Bible study and prayer are vital to our growth as Christians, whether we are new believers or have been following the Lord half our lifetimes. I have heard it said that if only the depressed Christian would "get into the Word," everything will be all right. But it does not follow that more Bible study and prayer are what the depressed Christian needs. Those who minister to the depressed must be careful about this. Depression can cause exaggerated emotions such as guilt that are out of proportion to reality.

Please be careful not to insist that the depressed Christian read the Bible and pray more. Bible study is usually impossible in major depression; often even Bible reading is too difficult. The inability to concentrate on the Bible does not prove that the person is unspiritual—but it may seem like that to him or her, and guilt could be increased.

Some of the coldest comforters, I have found, are those who use the Bible as the letter of the law instead of in the Spirit of the Lord, which is the same as the Spirit of the Word: "The letter kills, but the Spirit gives life" (2 Corinthians 3:6). I must risk being misunderstood and say that if Bible reading and prayer make the patient worse, they should be suspended for a time. Legalistic Bible study and prayer can impede recovery. The depressed Christian belongs to the Lord, who knows the hunger and thirst for righteousness of His sincere child. In time, as health returns, and if that child of God is ministered to in the love of the Lord Jesus, he or she will regain the desire and discipline for the Bible and prayer.

Helping to Carry the Burden

As the Christian community, let's seek to learn together. How refreshing it is that many Christians want to help and want to learn how to do it.

One morning I spoke to the university students at one of the weekly chapel meetings and was encouraged by a response later from a young woman student. Although I have much to learn, she was willing to learn even from me.

"Mrs. Moore, since the day you spoke in chapel, three of my friends have told me they are struggling with depression. Two of them shared very deeply with me, and it was then that your chapel talk meant the most to me. I remembered what you said about accepting, understanding and praying for them. And it made my ministry to them all the more effective."

It is almost 35 years since I left England to assist in mission work around the world. Never have I received so many letters, telephone calls or (these days) e-mails, or conducted so many private talks on the subject of depression. I am not a professional, nor am I doing anything special. I am just a Christian seeking to follow the Lord. If you have not reached out to the depressed, please know that much blessing can await you if you do.

The following letter from a woman named Kristen touched me. Even a little done in Christ's name can help more people than we imagine. The kind of gratitude expressed in her letter is waiting to be expressed by countless more. So many people suffer from depression that thousands more of us Christians need to be involved in helping thousands more Kristens:

> I want to thank you for confirming hope to my heart by your willingness to surrender to public speaking and surrendering your privacy by sharing your experience with clinical depression. I also believe there are many of us in this fast-paced world who live in such a "private hell" and need to hear the truth about a very real disorder, and the hope we could give of the answer God has provided. I thank you from the bottom of my heart for having the courage, and I pray that you will write your book and continue speaking so others like us can live the abundant lives God gives.
>
> Also, I would be very interested in any information you could recommend for me to understand more fully our condition so that I can speak to others with more authority. Being an introvert, I can be very intimidated, but with education I could overcome that. God bless you as the Lord uses you to minister to a very hurting world, and I will be praying for you that God will use you to help the ones He brings your way.

God brings many depressed Christians your way and mine. We do not all have the opportunity to speak in public, but things that may seem little can take more courage than public speaking. Don't underestimate the power of a warm greeting, for example, and a hug when appropriate.

Marybeth, a Christian women's leader in Nebraska, told me about a woman she suspected was depressed but who was hard to reach. Sally was not interested in talking and seemed rather cold. As most of us would be, Marybeth was reluctant to risk the woman's rejecting her efforts to help, but she decided to keep trying. It came to her that the next time she saw Sally, she should not say anything but simply put her arm around her shoulders. Later, when Sally was better and able to talk, she told Marybeth how much that gesture had helped her.

Not long ago I had a similar experience, able to do something small when I felt there was nothing at all I could do to help. A blonde, blue-eyed student came to visit my office. Deeply sad, she poured out her grief. Everything was hopeless.

How hard it is for the non-depressed to identify with hopelessness! Yet we must try. I started to reason with Rachel before I remembered that people in major depression cannot reason well. Then I started to quote some Scripture. She sighed and said, "I know."

When Rachel told me she needed to attend the university's biweekly chapel meetings but was too exhausted to get up in time in the morning, we agreed that I would call her dorm room for the next couple of weeks to wake her up in time to attend chapel. A little thing, perhaps, but the Lord can use little things.

Heavy-hearted for Rachel, I described her depressed anguish later that day (without using her name) to one of the university deans, a man who has known Rachel's kind of suffering.

"This is an institution of higher learning," I said. "Yet when it comes to an illness as devastating as major depression, no reasoning can help. Here we are, working hard to integrate faith and learning. But this young woman feels she is completely without faith. But she isn't. How can I help her?"

When I returned from lunch that day, I found a note from that dean, Dr. Mike Williams, slipped under my office door. Attached to it was a prose poem he had written at a time when he, too, had known the depths of depression.

Weightlifting

Galatians 6:2

It happened suddenly
before I knew it
the load became too heavy.

So heavy
I staggered
beneath its weight.

Each successive step on the journey
I seemed to stumble
with more and more efficiency.

It seemed obvious that soon
I would fall
flat on my face.

Crushed beneath a burden
my life wasted.
my heart broken.

So in terminal desperation
I cried out for help
from God.

My voice muffled
by the strain of a hardship
now bending my back
squeezing precious breath from my exhausted
     lungs
limited resolve from my feeble spirit.

God seemed not to hear.
Tears rolled down my cheeks

150

from the pain of the load
from the pain of a desertion
beyond my comprehension.

Clumsily I cried out again
shifted the ponderous burden.
God still did not come.

Then I saw you
standing beside me
with an almost helpless smile.

You placed your arm around me
shifted some weight to your own shoulders
not the heavy part but enough for me to know
that I wasn't alone.

The load no lighter, really
yet somehow more bearable
because you were there.

My steps somewhat more certain
because they were matched by yours
more certain because I noticed
there was a load on your back, too.

Still a bit troubled, though
Why had Christ not rushed to my side?
Did He ignore my agonized plea?
Frustrated still, and a bit uncertain.

I turned and saw you again
your load and some of my load
shared upon your shoulders.

The glass became clearer
for when our eyes met
I saw not your face
but the face of Christ.

The Loved Ones of the Depressed

"Do not fear, for I am with you; do not be dismayed, for I am your God. I will strengthen you and help you; I will uphold you with my righteous right hand."

Isaiah 41:10

One of my colleagues on staff at Dallas Baptist University is a mother and grandmother to whom I shall lend the name Fran. She is a mature Christian who takes joy in encouraging others and maintains a good sense of humor. One day Fran sent me a note:

I am glad to learn you are writing a book on depression and Christians. I have lived with seriously depressed folks most of my life. It is so tiring. Will your book contain a chapter for the family members of depressed people and for the caregivers?

Deciding that Fran must know much more than I about how to help the family of the depressed, I asked if she could meet me for lunch one day. Given her equable and optimistic out-look, I was surprised to learn that Fran's life contained a lot of tragedy.

After the birth of their three children and several years of controlling and irrational behavior, Fran's husband deserted her and the family. Only after his death many years later did Fran learn that he had been diagnosed with major brain dys-function, with accompanying major depression.

Her younger son died suddenly when still a young child one Christmas Eve after an illness of one day. Years later her other son, 21 years old, newly engaged to be married and a delight to Fran, died with his fiancée when a truck pulled out in front of his car not far from home.

Fran now shared her home with her adult daughter, Teresa, and Teresa's eight-year-old son. She told me she was very concerned for Teresa, who stayed in her room, had symp-toms of depression and refused to get help, saying simply that life had treated her harshly.

I was astonished that this co-worker of mine should be bearing such deep grief without disclosing a hint of it. There are two reasons I should not have been astonished. First, Fran loves God and has accepted what He has allowed in her life without bitterness. And second, because I know from many statistical sources that depression and deep loss are part of many households surrounding all of us.

Wondering how I could help Fran, I decided to enlist the help of some friends who have been praying for me in the writing of this book. I sent them an e-mail giving an update on the writing and telling them that I had been asked to write a chapter called "The Loved Ones of the Depressed."

"This is proving difficult to write," I told them. "I don't want to write a chapter full of pat answers when the situa-tion in every family dealing with a depressed loved one is dif-ferent. Does anybody have any ideas? If you have any expe-riences or insights you can share, will you please e-mail me back?"

How Do You Deal with Frustration?

An energetic co-worker named Kerry responded with four questions. Here is her first:

"What do you do when your husband or wife is depressed and you are dealing with frustration—at the person, at the situation, at the fact that God has not healed him? Who does the spouse talk to?"

Our wisest course is always to talk to God first. Surrender the situation to Him. I respectfully plead with you to do this first, and quickly. Accept the turmoil as something God has allowed. Give it to Him consciously, aloud or silently, on your face, on your knees or seated. Tell the Lord that you greatly need His help in trusting Him with a situation that is far too much for you to handle. Give up any right you may feel you have to a frustration-free or easier life. (Frustration means having an expectation neutralized, counteracted or disappointed. That which was hoped for or expected did not come to pass. Something prevented it. Now, a plan can be frustrated, but how can a person be frustrated? Especially when our expectations have been given to the Lord in surrender?)

Meet with God alone in a quiet place and humble yourself before Him. Don't leave that place until He has talked to you and you have heard Him. Ask Him to show you what to do. Then start watching and waiting immediately for specific guidance. Expect Him to act. He will act.

Who else should a person talk to when frustrated by living with a depressed mate? Let experts talk to you in print. Inform yourself about depression. It is hard work, but do not put off this vital task of educating yourself. Read, read and read. In preparing this chapter I was helped by the book *What to Do When Someone You Love Is Depressed* by Mitch Golant and Susan K. Golant. This and a few other sources are listed in the Recommended Reading list on p. 201.

The gaining of knowledge, as far as it is available at this moment, is essential. Without it you will remain distressed, and your loved one's recovery could be long delayed. There is much reading matter available. Ask God to lead you to exactly the right sources and material for you. If it is possible for you to talk to a counselor about the subject of depression in general, do it. If you know somebody who has recovered from depression, ask if he or she can help you understand more about it.

Accept with resolution, in faith, the fact that you are your depressed husband's [wife's, brother's, sister's] keeper. You have responsibility in that person's well-being (not *for* that well-being, as this would eliminate the loved one's own responsibility). This responsibility means we must help our loved ones and be Christ to them as much as we are able. We need to ask God, in prayerful time spent in His presence, to show us the kind of help our loved one needs. Let's ask God for the heart of a servant who is willing to learn to act in the Spirit of Christ.

Prepare for long-term blessing. The wisdom and practical love God will give in answer to that prayer will be the first steps on a much longer and wider road. On that road we will recognize many others who are not close relatives or friends but who are depressed strangers of whom the Lord will one day say to us, "I was sick and you looked after Me."

Ask God to show you the right person or persons in whom to confide, and then do it. There is no need to broadcast this depression, but do not try to keep it secret. If you feel you cannot confide in anybody, please take time alone with God to find out why. Go deeply into the matter with Him. Be very honest with God. Ask Him if pride is keeping you from doing the best you can for your depressed loved one. One of the best things you can do for yourself, and therefore for the other person, is to confide in somebody you trust.

If God has not given you a reason you should keep the matter secret, choose a person you can trust to pray and think with you—somebody who is empathetic (who has learned to view situations objectively) rather than unhelpfully sympathetic (one who commiserates too much). A small amount of sympathy can be helpful, but it needs to be closely watched. It can paralyze us by making us think our situation as caregiver is unfair. Empathy is far stronger and healthier. It can be robust and energizing and help move the frustrated caregiver into healthier attitudes and actions.

How Do You Deal with Guilt?

Kerry had a second question regarding how the loved ones of the depressed can be encouraged:

"How does the family deal with guilt—that they are to blame, that they need or want a break, that they are exhausted from the person and the illness?"

Guilt, as we defined it earlier, is the result of having done something wrong. Has the caregiver really done something to cause the illness in the loved one or to prevent his or her recovery? Perhaps this is the case. Ask God to show you if the guilt is real in His eyes. He will answer you. If He shows you that you are guilty, ask His forgiveness and cleansing, go to the person involved for forgiveness, then ask for the Holy Spirit's power to help you never again to do that wrong thing.

But if you are not guilty, then what you are feeling is false guilt. Do not blame yourself for something you are not responsible for. It uses valuable energy that can be applied toward the healing of your loved one.

How does a person deal with "guilt" that they want or need a break? Everyone in a care-giving situation needs a break at some time. We are no stronger than the disciples to whom Jesus said, "Come with me by yourselves to a quiet place and get some rest" (Mark 6:31).

It is interesting to note, however, that when they arrived at their place of anticipated rest across the Sea of Galilee, there was no immediate break. The crowds had beaten them there and were waiting for them! I believe we must accept, exhausted though we may feel, that rest may not be given at the time we think we need it. If we ask God for it, and in faith expect to receive it, rest will come at His appointed time.

A feeling of guilt, however unjustified, can arise from the apparent falling apart of the caregiver's once-orderly life. We may have the feeling that our inability to cope is forcing us to the desire for a break in caring for our depressed loved one. But what is a break? As long as she or he is ill, we will always be concerned, however short or long a time we are away. And how long a break is needed to restore rest and perspective? This is a matter each individual must work out for herself very deliberately with the Lord.

The only true rest is found in walking minute by minute with Him. And the only way to carry out that walk is to let the Holy Spirit have control of each part of us. I long for this and have much to learn, but I believe that some form of a particular prayer—"Fill me anew with Your Holy Spirit, please, Lord"—should be made several times a day. If we will only ask, we will receive.

In order to maintain the needed sense of coping, the loved ones of the depressed should try to maintain as many of the following kinds of activities as time will allow:

- Preserve routine. This helps maintain a sense of having life under control.
- Continue with hobbies or activities that bring relaxation.
- Be careful to maintain physical health. Walk in the fresh air and sunlight whenever possible. Keep up your routine at the gym or wherever you take your regular exercise.
- Keep a journal. Many people pour out thoughts and longings and prayers on those pages. I keep a diary, but for me it has always been a record of events, colors, sounds, sights and responses, not feelings. It helps me track events. For many it can help track progress in health recovery. I certainly recommend keeping a journal, but must confess that in my own case I let the writing of it

lapse during my recovery, especially during the time I was learning that I could be legalistic about this decades-long daily activity. I then let the writing lapse for a while.

- Maintain friendships. Former First Lady Rosalynn Carter writes in her book *Helping Yourself Help Others*:

You may feel as if your life's course is now dictated by the whims of your dependent one's illness. This is truly frightening. When caregivers perceive themselves as being alone and in "second place" with no one to talk to or help out, they often feel trapped—literally imprisoned in their own households. These feelings can lead to intense anger and depression, which can further drive away friends and family.

Reassure Them with Love

Kerry had a third question in response to my query about how people like Fran, my colleague whose life has seen so much tragedy, deal with depression in loved ones:

"How do family members deal with their own need to laugh and have joy, yet know that their loved one cannot join in?"

Although the depressed relative or friend may not be able to take part in audible or visible ways, there may be an inner joining in, or at least a longing for it, that we cannot perceive. Let's do all we can to help people know they are loved, respected, accepted and wanted. Each of us has the need to know we belong.

Here are some ways we can reinforce the fact that our depressed loved one is extremely valuable and part of the family. Even though he or she may not feel this, because of out-of-control emotions, the continual extension of true love is the strongest power on earth. With God's help let's seek to do the following:

- Reassure them—since the depressed often feel unloved and unwanted, and fear abandonment by those they love—that their greatest fears will not come about, and that we will always be there for them. (They are plagued with other fears and anxieties, too.)

- Explain to them that we may not have been through clinical depression ourselves, but that we are seeking understanding and want to help them.
- Reassure them that there is hope. Life will not always be this overwhelming. One day they will look back on it and say, "Remember when?" A friend of mine who was severely depressed some years ago heard these never-forgotten words from her counselor: "If you do not have any more hope, borrow mine. I have a lot of hope for you." The day came when hope was restored. But even before that day, she read and held onto this verse: "May the God of hope fill you with all joy and peace as you trust in him, so that you may overflow with hope by the power of the Holy Spirit" (Romans 15:13).
- Be silent often when you are with the depressed person. We have few answers to their disturbing questions, and talking can make an exhausted, depressed person more tired. Empathetic silence communicates that "I am here. I am listening. I care." So look and listen.
- Feel free to laugh. If the depressed person has been reassured of love and belonging, family members will be able to find outlets for the expression of laughter and joy without feelings of guilt. Concern for the loved one and longing for his or her feelings is normal and cannot be avoided. But feelings of guilt can.

As well as seeking to do and say the right things to their depressed loved ones, family members must also ask the Lord for help in not doing certain things. Examples are:

- Don't ignore the problem in a loved one, thinking, *It will pass* or *It's just a phase.*

159

- Don't take it personally if your loved one lashes out at those nearby. View it as part of their release mechanism during a difficult illness. The depressed person feels that life is controlling him, rather than that he is controlling life. Lashing out may give some unreal sense of power at a time when he is feeling powerless, helpless and hopeless.

- Avoid thinking, *If only she'd get her mind off herself.* Although taking responsibility for the welfare of others often seems to stave off depression once she reaches the point of being clinically depressed, your loved one cannot focus on others again until she is well.

- Do not try to reason with the severely depressed. It is impossible to reason with someone who cannot do so, so don't waste time trying. Logical thought has taken flight for a while.

- Don't take on too much responsibility and become an "enabler"—behaving in a way that makes it possible for an individual to continue with his or her problem or allow it to go untreated.

It may be difficult to be lighthearted in the presence of a loved one who cannot join in at present. And while that person is still depressed, the caregiver will always experience sorrow as well as longing that things were as they once were. But the discipline of carrying on with life must be maintained.

When Do You Step In?

Here is Kerry's fourth question:

"How does one recognize the line between letting God deal with the loved one and stepping in to take action yourself?"

Since clinical depression is a debilitating illness requiring treatment, frequently in the form of medication, it is very important that the depressed person be advised or urged to see a doctor.

Recently I saw that Betty, an elderly acquaintance who had just lost her husband of more than fifty years, was in the kind of depressed state that probably needed a doctor's help. Since she is a strong-minded woman, I debated with myself about whether I should recommend she see a doctor. Deciding I had nothing to lose and that Betty might have a lot to gain, I talked to her—tactfully, I hope—about some symptoms I had noticed that concerned me.

She was not sleeping or eating well and had withdrawn to some degree from her friends. Half-expecting her to refuse to see a doctor, I was glad when she agreed that she was not feeling right and said she would make an appointment that very week. Betty followed through, talked to her doctor and took the medication he prescribed, until he told her it was no longer necessary. Senior adults are often more pliable than we think, and we must summon our courage and speak up when we can see that help is needed.

On the other hand, as we all know, some depressed people steadfastly refuse to go to a doctor. I think of a senior adult couple who married fairly late in life. Mel, partly as the result of an illness, developed severe depression and stubbornly held out against seeking a doctor's advice. He was continually morose and became increasingly difficult to live with. His wife, after trying to ride the storm for several years, lost her own health. Divorce was the tragic result of Mel's refusal to seek professional help; he believed his depression was solely a spiritual problem in which medical science should have no part.

What does the family of a depressed young man do when he returns home unable to keep on with his job, and therefore unable to maintain his apartment or car? At first his parents or siblings may hope he will soon be well and able to be on his own again. But what if that does not happen and the son withdraws into his own world, staying in his room and not communicating with his loved ones?

"I can't ask Sam to leave," one widowed mother told me recently. "He would hate me forever." Then she added slowly, "But he says he hates me now, so I guess it wouldn't make much difference."

In cases like this I urge the caregiver to seek professional advice and counsel for herself. There are ways that have proved effective in setting reasonable limits to a loved one's behavior. This creates safety and allows the loved one to know what behavior is unacceptable or even life-threatening. If at all possible, do seek that help. Ask for help at church in finding a counselor, or ask a friend you think may know of a good source to pursue. And keep praying urgently that God will intervene. Ask Him, too, to break the power of Satan in the sufferer's life.

I am encouraged by the following account from a woman named Joy who attended a meeting at which I spoke in Southern California:

> My husband, Jim, suffered from cyclical depression for all 32 years of our marriage. As he became older, the depressed periods lasted longer and longer. About fifteen years ago he became a Christian and was better for a while. But then he started medicating himself on and off with alcohol. This was very hard for me and our children. My husband's anger grew, and he regressed in the Lord.
>
> One Sunday I prayed earnestly and urgently that Jim would be set free from Satan's grasp. There came a difference that both he and I noticed. Soon he allowed me to go to the doctor with him. Jim was given medication and almost immediately felt a change. In two days I saw a difference. Two weeks later he told me that perhaps he should have taken medicine 32 years ago.
>
> For the first time since we married, I feel happy.

What if your loved one does not, like Jim, agree to seek medical help, and you are concerned that he or she may be a danger to himself or others? This would, of course, be a final resort, but in some cases, after all else has failed and after much prayer, the severely depressed person must be committed, under protest, to a mental health facility. One person, Amber (whose hair color matches her name), told Carey and me that in the long run she can say she is glad her family took this action. In spite of her initial resistance, Amber is now grateful that she received the help she needed.

When I wrote that e-mail to my praying friends, asking them to advise me about helping people like Fran who have gone through much tragedy, I also received a response from Lucy:

> Two months ago our family had to have our aunt committed to a mental hospital. The supervising doctor testified about two weeks into the commitment that she would never be able to live alone again and would always need to live in a mental health facility under supervision.
>
> Yesterday evening, however, I visited our aunt at her home east of Dallas. She has been released with a new vision for keeping her home and fixing up her surroundings so that she will be content for the time she has left. She is only 63 years old.
>
> That which had seemed impossible has become reality! There is always hope, miraculous hope. Our aunt is rejoicing in the family that has become so attentive since she has been released. In fact, she is pulling all of us together for some good times of fellowship.
>
> I guess what I feel impressed to say is this: Continual hope and family support seem to have been pretty strong factors in her recovery. I am sure these are well-known components of the process of recovery, but we have actually seen it lived out in our own situation.

It Takes a Team

I have had my co-worker Fran foremost in mind in this chapter. "How can we help her?" I asked some of my colleagues. Kerry responded by asking that we deal with questions like these: Whom does a person talk to when facing frustrations caused by living with a depressed loved one? How does he or she deal with guilt? What if the person, exhausted by the loved one and the illness, wants or needs a break? When is it time to take action? There are many more questions, of course. By seeking resources and informing ourselves, we can find answers and help.

We also know from Lucy's account of her aunt, restored to her own home from a mental health facility, that a family can gather around a loved one, all pull together and actually see the loved one rejoicing! There is always hope.

Now may I direct the following words to you, especially if you are in a situation similar to Fran's?

I want to go two decades back in my memory to the time when I spent seven years as companion to the elderly Corrie ten Boom. When we started traveling together, and later moved into a rented house in California, neither of us had any idea that her life full of speaking, counseling, writing, music, inquisitive thinking, discussion and enjoyment of the beauty outdoors was about to be exchanged for a very confining one. Instead of adventure and accomplishment in the normal sense, we were about to enter a world of paralysis and mystifying brain disorder. The stroke that took away normal life lurked just around the corner.

In my sorrow at the sudden loss of Tante Corrie's gifts of communication, I was comforted time and again by the line of that poem by Amy Carmichael: "In acceptance lieth peace." I had no idea how long this trial was to last, but I knew there could be no peace for me unless I accepted completely that God had allowed this difficult thing to happen. I was not to resign myself to it like a martyr, or submit to it like a slave, but to accept it. I was to learn that acceptance, like faith, is essentially an active thing. In arriving at this acceptance—and it took months—I had before me a speechless but still determined Corrie ten Boom. Her example helped me accept the loss that God had allowed to overcome her, and also to accept the confining changes that necessarily took place in my life. It was very difficult, and I often failed to appropriate the grace of God.

The duration of Tante Corrie's illness was nearly five years. You, Fran and many others like you may have been dealing with the illness of a loved one for far longer.

Because Corrie ten Boom's testimony had helped thousands of people, and because there is no stigma attached to suffering a stroke (although brain damage and depression are also involved), her condition was known to many. This resulted in a strong support system for her and for me. The Christian community in Placentia, California, where we lived, rallied around us and sought to meet every possible need.

For example, people volunteered to bring food, fix the furnace, decorate the house with flowers, pray with us and insist that I take some time away from the house to walk at the beach. I marveled again and again at the power of such pulling together. The burdens of the patient and her household became lighter, the volunteers enjoyed their work and the cooperation made us all happy. I had a great assurance that we were happy because God was happy.

Surely that kind of combined help is His will and brings Him pleasure. It is surely how we are meant to go through life—pulling together as a community. Hundreds of times during those years of Tante Corrie's illness and since, I have thought to myself, *If only every sick and elderly person could receive this kind of loving help. There would be far less loneliness, pain and fear.*

Although many years have elapsed since Tante Corrie's death, I still have in my mind various scenes of members of the Body of Christ meeting her needs and mine by using their varying gifts. I relive those scenes often and can still see the players on the stage. Some were extroverted, hearty and strong. Others were quiet, slightly built and slipped out quietly, not wanting to be noticed or thanked for their contributions. This is surely the way the Body of Christ is meant to work. This is what brings joy to the Father. And truly, the sight of the Body of Christ working in this way is one of the greatest earthly gifts God has given me.

Dare we ask God to give us a dream? Dreams that are from Him can turn into reality. What if all of us who love the Lord and want to help the depressed would ask Him to help us to identify and then relinquish the things in our lives that are not really essential? That would give us more time to see the great needs all around us. And what if we asked God to show us how to use the particular spiritual gifts He has given each of us to help those who are depressed and those who constantly care for them?

Then, Fran, these needs of yours (and many others) would be met:

- Somebody who knows much more about brain dysfunction than you do would come to counsel you, someone who knows the right words and actions to draw Teresa out of her room.
- Someone—or, better still, two people—would be your confidantes in prayer. Together you could pray regularly and claim from God, with deep respect, a healing that now seems impossible.
- Another person would bring you a complete meal now and then.
- Somebody would be available to walk with you or undertake your favorite hobby with you.
- Perhaps several people from your church could get together to discuss and pray about the kinds of things that help them in caring for a sick loved one. The Lord gives strength and courage through shared insights.

There may actually be several people in your congregation who have similar burdens to yours but who think they are alone.

- The stigma of mental illness would be reduced. People would be willing to talk about it and to bear one another's burdens.

The loved ones of the depressed are not meant to go it alone. It takes a team—a large team.

The Gift
of Brokenness

The path of the righteous is like the first
gleam of dawn, shining ever brighter till
the full light of day.

Proverbs 4:18

It has been my purpose in this
book to bring comfort and help to the depressed Christian, and to help Christians
who have never been depressed to see the
Lord Jesus in their depressed brothers or
sisters, and to look for ways to better care
for them.

I can identify with both categories above,
for I know from experience what clinical
depression is like; and I was also among
those Christians who tend not to get involved with the depressed, seeing their
problem as having a mainly spiritual base.
Not all never-depressed Christians are as I
was, of course. Many do help and care.

When I was about ten years old, I sat
one day in the small, square living room of
the rather damp house in which our family lived in Hastings near the English Chan-

nel. I pulled my chair as close to the blaze in the hearth as I could and began to read the children's section of the small postwar edition of a women's magazine my mother read each week. Finishing that section, I flipped through the rest of the magazine and came across this prose poem by Minnie Louise Haskins. I read it, read it again, then memorized it:

> I said to the man who stood at the gate of the year, "Give me a light that I may tread safely into the unknown." And he replied, "Go out into the darkness and put your hand into the hand of God. That shall be to you better than light and safer than a known way!"

There was homesickness in me for that kind of close relationship with God—but regret, too. I was unwilling to place my weak hand into God's strong one. I wanted to find my own way and not risk His leading me onto His choice of path for me.

But when I was 21 years old, after years of resisting Him, I admitted that God was God, that His way was best and that it must, therefore, be best for me. I remember clearly the weekend in March 1965 when I made as honest a prayer as I knew how to phrase of total surrender to His will, whatever that might mean in the future.

From that turning point I was led down a far more fulfilling and challenging path than I could ever have imagined, much less planned. In every speaking or writing opportunity that the following decades offered me, I underlined that the Christian's secret to victorious living and answered prayer is total surrender to the will of God. I still teach that, and pray I always will.

When God's path for me held clinical depression, I found myself trying to discover within myself (as I have described in the preceding pages) some unsurrendered thing that might have contributed to the illness. What could it be? I asked God for help in seeing and dealing with anything I had not entrusted to Him, but I could not find it. My life was not perfect, and God had and still has much to work in me before I am conformed to the image of Christ, but I could not find any obvious, willful lack of acceptance.

As I experienced and began to recover from clinical depression, it slowly dawned on me that God was not asking me for any new surrender. I had thought I must have something else to give Him. But I had nothing at all. All I could do was come to Him.

Of the many descriptions of the Lord Jesus in the Bible, in only one place does Jesus Himself, in His time on earth, tell us what He is like. It must be meant that we pay close attention to His words:

> "Come to me. . . . I am gentle and humble in heart. . . ."
> Matthew 11:28–29

The aim of God is to change each of us so that we become like Christ. Christ is humble. He humbled Himself. We must humble ourselves. Anything that causes us to humble ourselves before God, even though that thing may not be good in itself, must be for our ultimate good, because it can make us more like Jesus Christ and bring us a step closer to reaching God's purpose for us.

Clinical depression is a very humbling illness. The sufferer feels powerless to change the situation. He or she cannot apply a quick fix, nor even keep up with life, despite every effort. Strength is gone. I like to think that I am strong and that I come across to others as strong. But I am not strong. I must relinquish to God not only my right to be strong, but also my right to appear strong.

Can it be that at this time, when God has ordained that we should live, He is allowing the incidence of clinical depression to rise because it is humbling and has the potential, therefore, to make us more like His Son? Would many of us not learn to come to Jesus Christ and keep coming to Him, were our supposed strength not brought to the end of itself?

We have nothing to bring to the Lord. In the words of the beloved hymn "Rock of Ages," "Nothing in my hand I bring, simply to Thy cross I cling."

There are no bargains to be made with God. We must come, minute by minute, every day, to the Lord Jesus. He wants us to come and simply receive from Him. There is nothing to fear from Him. Jesus Christ is gentle and humble in heart.

Words of Comfort from a Friend

Part of God's will in our becoming more like Christ is that we help others on the same journey. May I share with you a letter I treasure? It is one I received in August 1996 during my leave of absence from work. It is from a colleague who was being healed from the same humbling disease and who could write with authority.

Dearest Pam,

What a blessing for you to have some time away from campus to rest and think! I am grateful that the university made this arrangement with you, though we will miss you while you are gone. I only just discovered your absence. Your office says you are open to receiving mail, so I hope this contact will encourage you.

Of course, now that I sit down to write this, I realize there is nothing to say. There are no words that can fix your pain. There is no magic kiss that makes boo-boos stop hurting. Well, maybe that's wrong. There *is* one magic kiss that heals hearts, and that is the kiss of our Savior. But it takes time, and rest, and tears, and quiet, which I hope you are now experiencing.

Perhaps I should say only that I've been where you are, I know how it feels, I am recovering, and so know that healing can occur. For me healing is taking sleep, prayer, medication,

171

time away from work, reordering priorities and the same character growth we all need. You have the additional luxury of a
husband who loves you and will hold you physically, even as
our Lord holds you spiritually, right? What I call "cuddle time"
is a great joy that God provides to us women; let it be part of
your healing. And for me, beginning to heal took a crisis. I
wasn't ready to admit my need for healing until I was truly
desperate. Perhaps you have met your crisis.

Let the crisis be O.K. Let it take you down emotional roads
you never knew were there. Let it forge a new depth of love
and communication between you and Carey. Invite it. Rest
in it. Explore it. Let it do its work in you until the pain that
the enemy created to confuse you becomes the very thing the
King uses to redeem you emotionally. It feels so good when
God redeems the suffering and turns it into joy. The best
things that ever happened to me all started with pain and
ended in joy. That's the beauty of redemption, isn't it? It's
not just that God causes good things to come *out of* bad
things. It's that the bad things *become* the good things. Not
only do our evil natures become good natures through
redemption, but bad relationships become good ones; bad
societies become godly ones; bad conversations turn productive; bad institutions become the pillars of the community; and bad emotions turn into character and strength and
well-ordered priorities and deep relationships and intimacy
with the One who understands those emotions. And then,
ironically, all that turns into happiness.

We are blessed to be emotionally delicate, Pam, for we will
know a secret of joy that others never learn. We will know in
a way that others cannot know how God turns weakness into
strength, humility into peace, dependence into intimacy and
sorrow into genuine joy. We will understand redemption in
a way that many never do, for we *feel* our need for redemption in a way that many never do.

We are aware of the moment-by-moment redemption that
must take place in our hearts and minds and bodies if we are
to remain afloat in the overwhelming tide of emotional exhaustion that threatens to drown the weary women we are. Everywhere there is desperation, everywhere there is weakness,

everywhere there are tears, everywhere there is exhaustion, everywhere there is biochemical imbalance—in all those places there is the opportunity for redemption. And I now believe that experiencing redemption *is* the key to happiness. So, just as you and I may be biochemically disposed to sadness, we are, therefore, spiritually disposed to deep happiness—so long as we keep letting the pain drive us to the Redeemer.

O.K., so I had a little bit to say. And here's a little bit more. When I read your book *Safer than a Known Way,* I remember chuckling slightly every time you reported how Tante Corrie would say that the work always comes first. I know what she meant, so I hope she'll forgive me for picking on that statement, but I don't think the work always comes first with God.

To be sure, there is much work to do, and work is an inherently good thing, not a bad thing. But God created and redeems all of life. God is the God of work, but He is also the God of rest, of relationship, of quiet, of celebration, of health and even of the sensual (food, beauty, music, color, nature, art, etc.). Each of these must be present in our lives if we are to live as God intended. It's not just that these things keep us going so we can do the work. These things are part of the work of being human. To participate in rest and pleasure is to redeem those activities for the Kingdom—just as participating in our work at the university is to redeem souls and minds for the Kingdom. To neglect *any* of these things is to neglect our stewardship of God's plans. And to neglect any of these things is to despise who God made us to be and to despise who God is, since we are made in His image.

This is not to say that you have neglected these things. But you and I are very hard workers, and it took my own crisis for me to stop feeling guilty about participating in the rest of life. I'm guessing you're much the same. If God had meant literally for the work always to come first, He wouldn't have made creatures who are designed to sleep eight to ten hours of every 24. He meant for there to be a balance of work and rest, pain and pleasure, noise and quiet, crowds and solitude, work and play, the public Pam and the private Pam.

So don't worry about being gone during this time. Don't fret about what is not getting done. Don't feel apologetic that you must retreat for a while. We war-weary women need to restore some balance. We must return to Eden to remember what God intended life to be like in the Kingdom. We are in a bigger hurry than He seems to be much of the time. Even Jesus withdrew from the crowds to sleep, and He spent lots of time dining and laughing and praying and being quiet with His closest companions.

This is your time. Embrace it and let it restore some balance to life. Use this time to redeem the other parts of your life, and let God worry for now about the work.

Forgive me for sounding preachy. God has comforted me with these truths through my own battle with depression, and I wish only to comfort you as He has comforted me. He didn't bring you through all the extraordinary events of your life just to have you defeated by a little cancer or a little chemical imbalance or insomnia. He'll see you through this, too. Rest, dear friend. And sleep, and eat, and cuddle, and talk to Carey, and listen to God, and take your medicine, and do five things just for fun that you've never had time for before. And when you're through "doing," just practice "being" for a while.

Above all, don't listen to too much advice from friends like me who want to help but don't know how, so we clumsily try to comfort and encourage. Just know that you are loved by many patient people who expect nothing from you except for you to wait quietly in the presence of God while He redeems this part of Pam.

Warmly,
Debbie Moreland

Walking Hand in Hand into the East

If you are a depressed Christian, I want this book to help and comfort you. Although you may have no hope, healing can come. I know this because it has come for others. I have experienced it, too, humbling though clinical depression was and sometimes still is. My friend Debbie, in her letter to me in 1996, was receiving healing, too. Again, that was humbling. But when depression drives us to closer dependence on the

Lord Jesus, it is a good thing. The more He humbles us, the better we can know Him because He is humble. It is only through humility that we can know God. Above all we must know God and that He is absolutely good and trustworthy.

"I want to comfort you," wrote Debbie, referring to 2 Corinthians 1:3–4, "with the same comfort I have received." And comfort me she did! What a testimony to God's power, that a devastating illness like depression can turn into a good thing, through which someone like Debbie can bring much good to others.

Not all of us have a writing gift like Debbie's, but we, too, can find ways to comfort others with the comfort we have received. It is probably true most of the time that those who have suffered similar pain and loss are better able to help others going through the same thing. But those who have not experienced the same kind of pain can and must help, too.

During my recovery I tried to follow Debbie's advice to enjoy all parts of life. I had time to contemplate some poetry, and read again M. L. Haskins' prose poem about the man "at the gate of the year" who declined his inquirer's request to be given a light so that she could tread safely into the unknown. The man advised her to step out into the darkness with her hand in God's hand. That would be "safer than a known way."

But this time I read the next lines of the poem, ones I had not memorized forty years before:

> So I went forth and, finding the hand of God, trod gladly into the night. And He led me towards the hills and the breaking of day in the lone East.

Having received that admonition to relax, I indulged my love of contemplation, reflection and imagination. I remembered how, as a young woman, I had wanted a light to shine on the future, but was led instead to trust God by stepping out into the darkness and letting Him lead me. He had not failed. His hand holding mine had been better than light, safer than a known way.

But here I was, decades later, in a clinical depression that had robbed me of the desire to keep on with the journey. It was not that I had stopped trusting Him; I was simply too tired. Had I taken an unfortunate sidetrack off the right road?

Even as that question formed in my mind, I was sure I had not gone off the path. This difficult experience was part of the journey. Clinical depression was not to be the theme of the rest of my life's journey, but it was an important part nevertheless.

I continued to reflect on the last lines of the poem: "And He led me towards the hills and the breaking of day in the lone East." God's hand led the inquiring girl toward the hills and to the dawning of day. The picture of the two walking hand in hand is an intimate one. At the end of the story, you and I must have that trusting relationship with God alone, with no holding back or faltering. But in reality the scene is not a lonely one. The fact is, there are crowds of us walking together toward the shining light of daybreak. We need the Lord first and most, but we desperately need one another, too.

Even if a Christian has not experienced depression, he or she can help those going through it. There is only one way to do that, though. It is by humbling ourselves before the One who says we should learn from Him because He is gentle and humble in heart. He wants to show us the way to help those who are weak through depression. The weak can become stronger for the journey when, through other Christians, they receive the practical love and help of God.

Beyond the hills and the ever-increasing light of daybreak shines a more vivid light than we can imagine, and a Savior who longs to say to us:

"Come, you who are blessed by my Father; take your inheritance, the kingdom prepared for you since the creation of the world. For . . . I was sick and you looked after me. . . ."
Matthew 25:34–36

Facing Issues from the Past

In chapter 4 I introduced you to a woman named Cindy, who suffered for a year with severe clinical depression. I pointed out that while depression does not always have a specific spiritual root, there may nonetheless be spiritual reasons for it. Cindy discovered this reason—anger over her past traumas—and looked to the Lord to help her deal with it. Here is what she wrote me after a conference in which I recounted my own diagnosis of depression and invited others to share theirs.

Burying the Past in a Box

My background is one of traumatic abuse, rejection and confusion over my place in the world. I received this abuse from two very misguided people when I was young and impressionable.

Then, when I was fifteen, I gave my life to the Lord wholly and completely. It was such freedom for me! Never having known unconditional love, I let go of everything I had held onto in order to understand God's love. Once I met the Lord, all the abuse and rejection and confusion seemed to vanish— or so I would have liked to believe.

When I was 21 I moved to another state and became active in church through prayer and fellowship. I was popular for my charisma, energy and "spiritual depth." People seemed to gravitate to me for prayer and encouragement. I loved it! In all the glitter of popularity for my relationship with the Lord, I met a great guy to whom I was particularly attracted. He felt the same about me. We dated and were married within five months.

Our marriage started out with great excitement and energy. In only six months, however, my life changed. I still do not know exactly what triggered it, but depression hit like a bolt of lightning. Sometimes the newly married begin to see things in themselves that they have never seen before. Anger flared up in my heart and flew out of my mouth and fists before I was able to control it. I decided to see a counselor to explore this anger. *God forbid,* I thought, *that it continue in our marriage and be passed down to any children we might have!*

As the counselor and I explored the possibilities, it became clear to me that the root of my rage was buried deep in my past—the past I had thrown away and pretended had no more effect on me after I met the Lord.

While I was digging into particular memories and feelings, another symptom appeared, apart from the overwhelming anger: tiredness. I did not wish to go anywhere. I wanted my husband all to myself and asked that he stay home with me. I longed for life to slow down; everything was moving too fast. The tiredness grew into extreme fatigue. I could barely stay up during the day, and I looked forward to five in the afternoon, after work, when I could go home and sleep. I could handle that for a while, but life became more and more disorderly.

Depression began to disable me completely. My sleep suffered greatly. I had haunting thoughts of how lowly I was, how God must be paying me back for my birth. Isn't that horrible? I often look back on it now and get chills. Feeling utterly abandoned by God, I began to suffer mentally. My dreams were full of sickness and destruction. When I woke up I found little comfort. My husband was always right beside me, yet I was shut in the prison alone. My very existence began to torture me; I felt I was rotting in a deep, dark box.

The changes in me must have appeared astounding. I had been a young woman with much energy and hope in the Lord. Now I was reduced to a feeble, fragile shadow. My speech became slurred, my hands fidgety and my eyes blinking unusually fast and often. I thought I was losing my mind. I took various kinds of antidepressants, yet they seemed to have the reverse effect on me. I tried praying every day, to no avail. God seemed very far away and would have nothing to do with me. I tried going to church to find comfort, but that did not help much.

Most people told me this was happening because I did not trust the Lord enough. Others said I was not "in the Word" enough. Still others tried to pray against demonic oppression in my life. These "helps" just dug me deeper into the grave.

Out of the Box

Then one Tuesday night at Bible study, I was weeping during a time of silence while we waited on God as a church. A man on the other side of the room stood up with a word from the Lord that spoke directly to my heart. He explained that I was in a black box, and that there was good news and bad news. The good news: The Lord was in the box with me. The bad news: I would have to stay there for a while. The man went on to say that there would come a time when I would look back on that box and not see the ugliness it now held for me. One day I would actually see it as beautiful.

As I listened, I was comforted slightly by the knowledge that the Lord knew where I was and was watching me. On the other hand, the thought that I would have to stay in the box for a while nearly overwhelmed me. I did not know if I could hold onto life much longer. But I went home that night clutching the promise and trying to muster as much hope as I could from it.

Over the next few months I went through a series of ups and downs as I was forced to deal with the issues that were not really behind me at all. I also did a lot of studying of God's promises in the Bible. They were all I had to hold onto.

The depression lasted one full year. I think I prolonged the agony of it by clinging to the premise that the problem lay in my faith. But as I went through that horrible time, Jesus met me. Yes, I had met Him when I was fifteen years old, but I had never let Him meet me. Many times, I realized, the Lord had spoken to my heart about dealing with the issues of the past, yet I was always too fearful to look at them.

I now know that Jesus Christ has a deep desire to heal us all from the inside out. If we lack the faith to deal with the issues on our own accord, He will push us through them sooner or later. Why? Because He is thorough with His work in us and leaves no loose ends.

The Desert
of Rebellion

In chapter 4, "Is Depression My Fault?", I also introduced you to a young student named Rebecca. I focused in that chapter on the understanding that depression is often not caused by deliberate sin. We all still sin, but if we are seeking to lead lives obedient to the Lord, He will help us to recognize daily, ongoing sin. When we do, we must ask forgiveness from Him, receive His forgiveness and step out afresh with the Holy Spirit. These are normal happenings in the Christian's life. We are works in progress, after all, still in the process of being conformed to the image of Christ. There are times, however, when deliberate sin does cause depression. Here is Rebecca's story.

Who Am I?

I was eleven years old when I buried my face in the back of an avocado green La-Z-Boy and asked the Spirit of the living God to enter my heart. My life after salvation was marked by outward peace as the Holy Spirit surrounded and covered me in all my spiritual endeavors. I was active in my church youth group, and God's presence guided me on mission trips, through Bible studies I led and in conversations as I worked to influence people toward the Lord.

But a storm was brewing in my heart, a black squall of rejection accompanied by severe feelings of oddity. I felt somehow that I did not fit in, that I was not equal with every other young woman I was growing up with. Underneath my candy apple coating of Christianity, I began to harbor desires in my heart that I was ashamed of and that I was terrified I might act on someday—desires for affection and sexual fulfillment from members of the same sex, desires to be cherished, loved and respected.

I was a soccer goalkeeper from age four, and played with the same team until I was a senior in high school. The team enjoyed a strong sense of unity, and my position meant that it was my job to defend the other girls. But as I devoted more and more time to soccer practice, my role as defender began to carry over into other facets of life.

I also overidentified with my father while I fought with and underidentified with my mother. She herself dealt with slight phobias, which I could not respect since I had begun to base my identity on fearlessness and bravery. Because of the aspect of the faith that encourages Christians to be adventurous and fearless, I felt that my personality had a place in church and that I could earn respect there.

During my adolescence I searched high and low for someone to love me just the way I was. I looked to boys first, but was always rejected by them and welcomed by my friends who were girls. As my search continued, I became increasingly beaten down and unaware of how to fellowship with the Holy Spirit for comfort and fulfillment. I knew I was divided in my heart, and hated myself for it, but I did not know how to change. I read my Bible and went to church in order to ease my conscience, but I was unable to find fulfillment emotionally.

Outwardly no one in the church would have ever guessed, but occasionally the melancholic side of my personality would let me dangle my feet in a growing undercurrent of rejection and mysterious desire. I halfway wanted to know this other part of me, but mostly hoped I would never make waves. I sensed, in this other side of me, the spirit of suicide and anger, rebellion, wildness, coldheartedness, deceit and violence.

On entering college I became friends with two churchgoing young women who accepted me since I was new to the school and they were farther along. But I was a fifth wheel, sometimes welcome and sometimes not. For two years I tried, but the moments I was welcome grew more sporadic. Eventually I quit going around to see them, and waited for the next set of friends to go through.

I had so many failed attempts at relationships by then that it hardly mattered. I felt like a frozen lake that had been skated on and abandoned.

Up until this time I had told only one or two people that I had lesbian desires. They loved me but did not know what to tell me, so I kept the issue bottled up and pretended I was O.K.

Everyone in the church I was attending treated me as if I mattered. I was outgoing and very involved, and felt I had to hide the issue of my confused sexual identity. God should at least *appear* to be enough for me; and I was good at the façade that I had been in fellowship with Him all my life. This was the only shred of self-respect I had remaining. Deep down, though, I felt that the Lord was disgusted with me and that I had already canceled His plans for me because of the hypocrisy I could not seem to fix.

Losing Myself

When I returned home from my first year in college, I sat alone on the weekends watching classic movies and drinking coffee. I wanted someone to come into my life and sweep me off my feet, but I was too self-reflecting, self-oriented, self-conscious, so I began to allow more than my feet to dangle in what was now a vortex of underlying shame and rejection and blackness. I was pulled in, and it was not long before I met a girl.

Beware that what you harbor in your soul you will draw unto yourself. We were both Christians, and we started our friendship in Christian conversation. Soon I discovered that she had the same problems as I did, with a different twist, and in time we were more than friends.

My heart was more divided than ever. I had finally found what I was looking for, but not without the abandonment of what I was meant for. My identity crisis came to a head. I had lost myself, but I was loved, whoever I was. Needless to say, my depression was deep. Anytime a person loses himself, there is no peace.

God proved His Word true. Numbers 32:23 says, "You may be sure that your sin will find you out." Our parents discovered the nature of our relationship and the truth was brought to light. My inner squall was made visible and the undercurrent became a tidal wave. All that I had been so careful to hide was laid open and I was terribly ashamed, fearing more rejection. The girl and I were not really happy together and we knew it, but even after being caught, we found ways to be together. We simply did not know how to change.

As justice would have it, we were again discovered, and each of us was removed from our parents' homes—not in anger, but in love, according to 1 Corinthians 5, in hopes that we would see our need to change. I deeply wanted to be healed, and so did she, so we agreed that I should move out of the area.

A couple who had served as youth ministers, whom I had told of my problem along the way, offered to take me in so I could recover. I moved to their small town in the country at the beginning of summer and lived in their home. If I had not been so carefully handled and made aware of God's unconditional love, I would surely have been lost in the undertow. But His love during that fragile time gave me hope and made me realize there was a possibility that I could change. God's unconditional love was my life preserver in the wreckage.

I owe so much to my former youth ministers that I could never repay them. I was on the bottom and did not know how to get up. I was not exactly full of energy to go out and meet new people in that small country town, so I did not have a lot of healthy Christian fellowship right away. Trying to give up, I called the girl and asked to come live with her. She told me no. I am thankful now that she did, but at the time I knew only one way to take it. Eventually she told me she did not want to hear from me again. I was crushed.

Then the depression began to manifest itself. I remember lying in bed at night trying to get to sleep. My soul felt far away from me. I saw myself on the edges of reality peering over at what lay below, and feeling that I might fall at any moment. These visions of my soul's demise were always accompanied by a piano playing faintly in the background. It was peaceful in an eerie sort of way, and almost enough to make me lose my mind. Frequently I woke up with dreams that gave me new ideas for committing suicide—clever ways so that no one would really know if it had been suicide or not. I was terrified that I might actually do something like that in my sleep.

I was always fatigued. I did not want to keep myself clean or meet anyone. I did not want to receive comfort or direction, nor did I want to go on with my plans to go back to a Christian school. I felt used up and miserable and could not fathom that God would be able or willing to do anything with me. In fact, I did not want to pursue life at all anymore. I did not know the person in the mirror, but would wake up some nights to find myself standing in front of it, crying so hard that my face was almost unrecognizable.

I was angry with God for dumping me off and tearing me away from the only romantic love I had been able to keep for any period of time. At the same time I felt sick at myself for having fallen into such sin. I felt alone and empty.

God's Onslaught of Love

I don't really know what the first thing was that began to work to bring me to repentance, except God's onslaught of love. He raised up an army of praying people who helped lift the veil from my heart's eyes so that I was able to grasp truth at an accelerated pace. But I still had a battle to fight. Physically I had stopped sinning; the relationship was over. But there were attitudes in my heart that were still sinful. Unless I came to the point where I was willing to agree with the Spirit of God, who was grieving over these sinful attitudes inside me, I would be bound to my depression.

When you are a Christian in outright disobedience of *whatever* nature, there is no cure for depression except repentance. This is because your heart is divided, and that division eventually forms a crevice in your life that continually widens to swallow you, and from which you cannot escape without divine intervention. God waits for our invitation, once we see that we are in need. He will take the necessary steps to show us our spiritual poverty. Then, once we see, He waits, and we have to ask Him to keep working and rescue us. If we choose to stay in the pit, we can—but being rescued requires some effort, some work at obedience. He simply stands and knocks, even on the door of the life of a Christian.

God had shown me that there was a way of escape, and He was knocking on my door, waiting to see if I would let Him back in.

This day I call heaven and earth as witnesses against you that
I have set before you life and death, blessings and curses.
Now choose life, so that you and your children may live and
that you may love the LORD your God, listen to his voice, and
hold fast to him. For the LORD is your life. . . .

Deuteronomy 30:19–20

He had removed me from the situation so I might have a
more objective view and see if I really wanted to follow Him.
He was patient with me through the grieving process of losing a loved one. Then He showed me, by the testimony of a
good friend I met through all this, that escape was definitely
possible. She had been in the depths of this sin herself for a
while, but was now married with a family, and God was bringing people to her to counsel through these issues.

Realizing that I needed a lot of healing, and that God was
not angry with me for misdirecting my needs for love, but
that He wanted to show me "the most excellent way" (1 Corinthians 12:31), I opened the door to Him. I told Him I
wanted to love and be loved in a pure way, and that I would
stay with Him because I knew He was the only One who
could love me perfectly.

Later, addressing my fear that God had walked away from
me and canceled any plans He had for me, Romans 11:29
would tell me that "God's gifts and his call are irrevocable."
He does not cancel plans—but we can walk away from them.
God never leaves or forsakes us. It does not matter that in
our heads we think He hates us. Rather, it matters that in His
Word He says He will go after the one lost sheep, not wait by
the ninety-nine who have not wandered. It matters that Jesus'
blood covers all our sins; that His grace will change us; that
our inefficiencies and doubts and hurts can be worked
through and actually used for good.

I want to say here that we as Christians need to practice
being so in tune with the Spirit of God that we can sense
when someone is in a fragile state and learn not to push him

or her to a decision. It might be fatal to that person, and the Holy Spirit is the only qualified agent for change; He alone truly knows when the heart is ready. Instead we need to embody the character of Jesus portrayed in Matthew 12:18–20 by God the Father:

> "Here is my servant whom I have chosen, the one I love, in whom I delight; I will put my Spirit on him, and he will proclaim justice to the nations. He will not quarrel or cry out; no one will hear his voice in the streets. A bruised reed he will not break, and a smoldering wick he will not snuff out, till he leads justice to victory."

After I reached up to God and made a choice, I had to address with Scripture promises every *what-if* question running through my mind, so that I would be firm in my decision. *What if I never marry because of this? What if she decides to take me back? What if I fall again with another person? What if everyone finds out? What if God wants me to use this for others and I have to talk about it? What if she never decides to change and I have to watch her develop other relationships?* Would I still find God to be enough, and choose Him? Could I ever agree wholeheartedly with Psalm 16 that tells of the boundary lines falling in pleasant places and be satisfied with the Lord as my portion?

This took a lot of time to work through, but the Father is patient, "not wanting anyone to perish, but everyone to come to repentance" (2 Peter 3:9).

James 4:8 says, "Come near to God and he will come near to you. Wash your hands, you sinners, and purify your hearts, you double-minded." I found comfort in this verse because I understood that I did indeed need to take the first step, but that in it I risked no fear of rejection from God. I was tired of stepping out into relationships because they always ended in rejection, while God promised that He would draw near to me—and nearness was definitely what I needed.

I also needed to put aside my questions with the sword of truth. This is the key to hope. What is hope? It remains, we know that. "And now these three remain: faith, hope and love." So what is hope? Revelation 21:5 summarizes it well enough: "He who was seated on the throne said, 'I am making everything new!' Then he said, 'Write this down, for these words are trustworthy and true.'" My hope lay in the fact that Jesus would overlook everything I had done, love me anyway and make my heart new. As expressed in Hebrews 7:19, "A better hope is introduced, by which we draw near to God."

I did this.

Grasping the Concept of Freedom

Even after the introduction of hope, however, I still had to deal with my depression. I had repented and made the decision to follow Christ, no matter what I lost, but my depression lingered. The Holy Spirit had to convict me in regard to my sin, but once I repented, I was still not free from the guilt. I had not distinguished between the conviction of God that causes a person to desire change and the accusations of the devil saying that I would never change, and that even if I did, I was still a disgusting person because of all the things I had done.

This is called condemnation, but Romans 8:1 says that, after repentance, we are released from the burden of condemnation: "There is now no condemnation for those who are in Christ Jesus." Psalm 103:12 says that God removes our sins "as far as the east is from the west." They are blown away! We need desperately to teach this to our brothers and sisters struggling to pray against the memory of their sin. It is theirs no more; it belongs to Christ. What freedom there is in that!

In fact, that is the key to taking hold of hope—when we forsake the lies we are told about ourselves and stand in grace, rejecting the condemnation of our souls and clinging to the cross of redemption. What is hope except that we are made new so we can be near to Christ? And where is Christ except at the right hand of God, constantly interceding for us at the throne of grace (see Hebrews 7:25)? "Let us then approach the throne of grace with confidence," Hebrews 4:16 encourages us, "so that we may receive mercy and find grace to help us in our time of need." And how can we approach the throne of grace with confidence if we do not shed the snakeskin of condemnation?

Even after repentance, depression lingers if we do not understand the freedom in forgiveness. It is vital that we grasp this concept, because no changes in a person can be made who is not standing at the throne of grace *confidently believing the promises*. And if no changes are made, the repentance is not genuine, leaving the person to drown in the despair of disobedience. It will be a vicious cycle until there is a breakthrough of grace.

Ephesians 2:8 says, "By grace you have been saved, *through faith. . .*" (emphasis added). Change comes only by believing! This is why Jesus tells us, "You will know the truth, and the truth will set you free" (John 8:32). God does not want us to live in turmoil. He wants us stable and secure. Hope brings security. Listen to Hebrews 6:18–20:

> We who have fled to take hold of the hope offered to us may be greatly encouraged. We have this hope as an anchor for the soul, firm and secure. It enters the inner sanctuary behind the curtain, where Jesus, who went before us, has entered on our behalf. He has become a high priest forever.

The fact is, we are meant to be near God, and He is always faithful to show us the way. We must flee from our sin in order to take hold of the hope—but if we do, our depressed hearts are to be *greatly encouraged*!

In the case of depression caused by rebellion, it is our choice if we will wander in the desert of depression for a prolonged period. The journey the Israelites took was meant to last only eleven days, but because of their unbelief they were unable to enter His rest for forty years. If you have disobeyed, you face a difficult road to recovery, but how long it will last is actually up to you.

If I wanted, I could wander right back into that wilderness any day I choose, but this time it would be deliberate sin, because I know how to be free. I could find a way back into my depression with meditations on the wrong ideas, because the kingdom of darkness forgives its deserters as well.

Such vulnerability can be overwhelming during the restoration process, and even the thought of defeat can bring on more depression. But the strength anyone needs to break free from depression caused by disobedience lies in meditation on the Word and promises of God. The clearer your picture of the character of God, and the more steeped in truth your heart is, the more likely you are to overcome.

Redeemed from the Pit

By God's grace I am doing well. I constantly use the truth God has revealed to me to intercede for my friends who need freedom as desperately as I did. I have learned to trust in God for all my needs—emotional, spiritual and physical. His Holy Spirit fills me, and I am constantly drawn to Him for times of nurturing in our relationship. He has restored me and given me a new love for life and a certainty in walking according to His plans for my life. I am free and full of the joy of the Lord, which is my daily strength. The first five verses of Psalm 103 truly speak my heart:

> Praise the LORD, O my soul; all my inmost being, praise his holy name. Praise the LORD, O my soul, and forget not all his benefits—who forgives all your sins and heals all your

diseases, who redeems your life from the pit and crowns you with love and compassion, who satisfies your desires with good things so that your youth is renewed like the eagle's.

Lord, I want to thank You for the resurrection power You have worked in me to raise my life from the pit of destruction. Fix my eyes for me on Your empty cross, and give me the endurance never to let my focus stray. Please accept this humble expression of gratitude that wells within my soul. Help me be ever grateful, for You have shown me that it is the powerful combination of humility, faithful expectation and grateful remembrance that releases me into Your grace, allowing me to become more like You, to draw near to You. Amen.

Appendix C

Springtime Came Late for Dorothy

Dorothy McManus Shellenberger, my "American mother," to whom I have referred in several places in this book, went through a serious depression in the early 1970s, when far less was known about the illness than is now the case. She wrote the following piece in 1980.

Life Turns Gray

Haden Hall is the name of the psychiatric ward in our hospital. "Haden Hell" was the name I gave it. This place where you were behind locked doors, no visitors except doctors and clergy (not even family at first). Empty-eyed and empty-purposed people sitting staring into the TV or walking up and down the halls or moaning in their rooms, their lives as fragmented

193

as the jigsaw puzzles they spent endless hours trying to reassemble. It was easy to spot the newly arrived lining up for meals: unkempt hair, extremely thin or obviously obese, no makeup or much too much, vacant eyes and dejected faces and defeated posture labeling their depression. *And I was one of them.*

January had been extremely bleak that year. Not cold enough to keep a laughing fire going in the den, but for days on end the sun refused to shine and the lake behind our house turned pewter gray. Our Mallard ducks, Lyndon and Lady-bird, disappeared just before Christmas, so there was no reason to go down to the lake each afternoon with corn and old bread crumbs and watch them fly in from some hidden spot in answer to my loud *quack, quack*. But the thought of our beautiful pets—so tame they would eat out of your hand—being lured away to provide the entrée for someone's Christmas dinner would cause me to burst into uncontrollable tears.

Other everyday problems mushroomed out of proportion, too. Telephone calls from our daughter in the East alarmed and frightened me. She and her husband were caught up in ideologies that were foreign to me. Our youngest daughter, away in school, was homesick and miserable, but she was determined to stick out the year. Our oldest son had recently embarked on a business venture much too ambitious for his young years, or so I thought.

Gradually, for me, life began to take on the pewter color of our lake. And as the grayness grew, the symptoms of depression spread. I stayed in bed. Charles, my husband, would fix his own breakfast, and when he came home for lunch, I was still not dressed, nor had I even cleared his breakfast dishes from the table. Food no longer tasted good, so I quit eating. My friends would call, I let the phone ring. They tried to visit me, I would not answer the door. Finally they quit trying.

I misplaced things—my glasses, my car keys, my check-book, my cup of coffee, the letter I was trying to write to one of our children. Then I would panic. Maybe I had thrown my glasses into the trash. Maybe someone had come into the house and stolen my money. What if Charles found out I had not paid all those bills? Rather than make any effort at all, I would go back to bed and pull the covers over my head.

I forgot food cooking on the stove, my beauty shop appointment, the party I was invited to, the telephone call I had promised to return, the board meeting I was supposed to attend, the cake I had promised to bake for the church bazaar. Or, if I did not forget, I made excuses. The car wouldn't start. I had unexpected company. I had a headache. The children were coming home. We were going out of town.

Charles made appointments for me to see our family doctor. I either broke the appointments or just did not show up. Gretchen, our faithful maid who had worked for us when the children were home, returned to full-time duty, arriving before Charles left for the office and staying with me until he was home for the night. For days on end I would not dress, staying in bed or lying on the couch gazing off into space, disinterested in everything.

I began to think of suicide. There was a gun in the wall safe, but Charles carried the key with him. Two boys had broken through a barrier at the end of the road at remote Willow Lake, submerging their car, but they had gotten out. The barrier had never been replaced. It should not be too hard if one gunned the motor a bit. I envisioned other ways—an overdose of pills, a slashed wrist—but something always stopped me. I thought it was cowardice; now I know it was something more.

On my last day at home, a friend came to see me and, against my explicit orders, Gretchen let her in. She came into my room bringing a beautiful red rose in a bud vase.

Concern etched her deep brown eyes. "Dorothy, darling, how are you?"

"I'm dead," I answered. "I'm emotionally, mentally, spiritually dead. Surely someone will realize it soon. Go away."

She left. But the minute she got to her own phone, she began calling all the members of her Bible study to solicit their prayers for me, for she recognized just how sick I was.

Charles realized it, too. Coming home a few minutes after she left that day, he came into the bedroom and sat down on my bed.

"Dorothy, I'm going to do what has to be done. I should have done it weeks ago. I'm calling our doctor and asking him to have you committed to the psychiatric division of the hospital."

And so I arrived at Haden Hall that winter night just as the steeple bells in the little church two blocks away were pealing out "Sweet Hour of Prayer."

The Gift of 1 Peter 5:10

The psychiatrist our doctor had referred me to came to the hospital and spent an hour with me. When he left he ordered the nurse to give me an injection so I could get some sleep.

Shortly after he left, a big man stationed himself just outside my door. Every five minutes or so he peered around the corner to see if I was all right. Once he came to the side of my bed, looked down at me and said, "Go to sleep, lady. You're going to be all right. I'm praying for you." I did not answer him and I did not go to sleep, but I'll never forget his compassionate words and his caring, soothing voice.

The days droned on. A bevy of doctors came to see me—an internist, a heart specialist (because of a functional heart disorder I had had since childhood), my psychiatrist twice a day, my husband as often as they would let him. But even though I had been a Christian and a church member for many years, my pastor never came.

One morning I did have a visitor. Not a human one. It came as a gift from the Great Physician. I was always so cold,

I had asked Charles to bring me a winter robe. He brought one that I did not wear often, a fine, quilted silk one that our Chinese "daughter" had sent me from Hong Kong. In the pocket I found a Scripture printed on a small card: "But the God of all grace, who has called you to His eternal glory through Jesus Christ the Lord, after that you have suffered a little while, will perfect you, establish, strengthen and steady you" (1 Peter 5:10).

All day long I repeated that verse. When they brought my tranquilizers, I took 1 Peter 5:10 along with my medicine. When I walked in the hall, I kept my hand around that small piece of cardboard in my pocket. I, who could not memorize anything anymore, was determined to memorize that Scripture—the first positive thing I had done in months.

When I went to the dining room, I repeated that verse before I ate. That night for the first time, I felt like praying. "Dear Lord, I never even knew 1 Peter 5:10 was in the Bible. But I'm claiming it for my verse. Whatever you want to do, Lord, however long it takes, I'm hanging onto *my* verse."

A week later my psychiatrist said that if Charles would take me away for a while, he thought it would help me get well. I did not think I was ready; the hospital had become a protective cocoon from the realities I would have to face once I was out. But Charles said a trip to Colorado would give me a chance to adjust gradually. Reluctantly I agreed to go.

The Piñon Pine

On May 15, 1972, Charles checked me out of the hospital and we headed west toward Colorado. Passing through the eastern edge of New Mexico, he suggested that we drive up Capulin Mountain.

Capulin Mountain is an inactive volcano and a national monument. From the rim of the crater, one can view the distant mountains of Colorado to the west, and look east to the

197

flatlands of west Texas, north to the panhandle of Oklahoma and even catch a glimpse of Kansas on the farthest northern horizon.

Around the rim of this large, well-preserved cinder-cone volcano is Crater Rim Trail. Charles, a nature lover and better-than-average photographer, wanted to take the mile-and-a-half walk around the rim's edge. I would rather have stayed in the car, but I went. There were so few things I had done in the last few months to please my husband.

Along the trail were numbered posts on both sides of the trail. We matched them to the numbers of the paragraphs in the trail guide booklet we had bought at the office, and learned about "a river of lava turned to stone" and "mountain mahogany" and "gambel oak" and "skunkbush."

Then, stopping at post number eleven, we examined a piñon pine.

The porcupines, using their large chisel teeth, tear off the tough outer bark of a small area and feast on the tender, succulent, growing cambium layer beneath. When they have had their fill, the sticky sap of tree comes out and completely covers the wound. It acts as a healing balm to protect the tree, and the porcupine moves on, leaving the tree, though wounded, protected from further hurt in that area.

Charles spotted a red-tailed hawk soaring high on the wind and went on up the trail to get a telephoto shot of him. I sat down on the bench by the piñon pine to wait. As I looked around, I discovered the scrubby, needled, evergreen piñons everywhere. Almost every one of them had suffered a porcupine injury, some more than one. But each was covered with the pine needles that smell so distinctive—a pungent, almost intoxicating fragrance. The piñon cones, containing tiny but tasty and highly nutritious nuts, were already beginning to form, and in the fall people would flock to Capulin to harvest them. These trees, though injured, were still growing and still productive.

Sitting quietly, breathing in the clean, piñon-scented air, I suddenly realized it was the Lord who had brought me to this place. I was like that wounded piñon pine. Depression, like the porcupine, had made an indelible scar on my life, but the healing sap of God's love that had been promised to me in that one verse of Scripture was flowing. Someday very soon I, too, was going to be established, strengthened and steadied, a useful, productive member of society again. God had given me the promise in 1 Peter and had shown me its fulfillment in these few, never-to-be-forgotten moments on the top of Capulin Mountain.

Charles was coming back down the rim's path, and I ran to meet him.

"Dorothy," he cried, "your face is shining. You are actually smiling! What has happened to you?"

"Oh, Charles," I said, "the long winter is over."

Breathlessly I began to share the experience of the last few minutes.

For a long time, in the solitude of that mountaintop, we clung together. Then, arm in arm, we continued our journey around the crater's rim with a new awareness of the faithfulness of God's Word, appropriated for our individual needs.

Recommended Reading

Publishing Resources

Barshinger, Clark E., Lojan E. LaRowe and Andres Tapia. "The Gospel according to Prozac." *Christianity Today*, August 14, 1995.

Bloomfield, Harold, and Peter McWilliams. *How to Heal Depression*. City: Prelude Press, 1994.

Burns, David, D., M.D. *Feeling Good: The New Mood Therapy*. New York: Avon, 1999.

Carlson, Dwight L. *Why Do Christians Shoot Their Wounded?* Downers Grove, Ill.: InterVarsity Press, 1994.

Carmichael, Amy. *Toward Jerusalem*. Fort Washington, Pa.: Christian Literature Crusade, 1977.

Carter, Rosalynn. *Helping Yourself Help Others*. New York: New York Times Books, 1996.

Golant, Mitch, and Susan K. Golant. *What to Do When Someone You Love Is Depressed.* New York: Villard Books, 1996.

Kramer, Peter D., M.D. *Listening to Prozac.* New York: Penguin, 1993.

Ten Boom, Corrie. *Defeated Enemies.* Fort Washington, Pa.: Christian Literature Crusade, 1991.

Thomas, Gary. "The Forgiveness Factor." *Christianity Today*, January 10, 2000.

Internet Resources

Website: <www.nami.org>. NAMI (National Alliance for the Mentally Ill), a nonprofit organization that advocates for research and services in response to major illnesses that affect the brain. NAMI helpline: 1-800-950-6264.

Website: <www.aacap.org>. American Academy of Child and Adolescent Psychiatry.

Website: <www.intelihealth.com>. Trusted information about health for every age group and member of the family, including depression in different age groups.

Born near London, **Pam Rosewell Moore** has lived in the United States since 1976. That year she became companion to Corrie ten Boom, the Dutch Christian whose incarceration in a Nazi concentration camp during World War II is known to many through the book *The Hiding Place* and the film of the same name. It was Pam's privilege to live and work with Miss ten Boom from 1976 until her death in 1983.

After seeing the victorious end to Tante (Aunt) Corrie ten Boom's life, Pam wrote her first book, *The Five Silent Years of Corrie ten Boom* (Zondervan, 1986). This describes the last years of the Dutch evangelist's life, when she was crippled and silenced by successive strokes, and it also relates Pam's reactions to those events. *When a person cannot achieve in the normal way, where does his or her value lie?* This is the question the book asks of a society in which a person's worth often seems related to personal achievement.

In 1988 Pam wrote her second book, *Safer than a Known Way* (Chosen), which tells of her growing up in Hastings, Sussex, England, and coming to know the Lord Jesus Christ when she was twenty-one. At that time she surrendered her own will to the will of God. Her previous reluctance to do so had lain in the fact that she thought he might want her to be a missionary—something she was sure she could never do. Missionaries were often required to do three things Pam knew were impossible for her—leave home and family, speak in public and lead a single life. But in the years following her prayer of relinquishment, she was to see the Lord fulfill her through the very things she had feared.

In 1966 Pam left England for a year of volunteer work as secretary to the Archbishop of East Africa in Nairobi, Kenya. In 1968 she joined the mission of Brother Andrew, God's smuggler, in the Netherlands. For more than seven years she saw God work miracles as teams transported Bibles and Christian books across the forbidding borders of Eastern Europe.

After her marriage to Carey Moore in 1986, Pam Rosewell Moore lived for two years in Waco, Texas, before the couple moved to Dallas in 1988. For the next fourteen years she worked at Dallas Baptist University, first as director of that institution's intercessory prayer ministry and then as director of spiritual life. Carey is Government Documents Librarian at Dallas Baptist University.

In 1991 Pam and Carey wrote their first book together. *If Two Shall Agree*, published by Chosen Books, addressed the need for Christian couples to pray together. This book was re-released in 1999 under the title *What Happens When Husbands and Wives Pray Together?*

Pam, who speaks often at conferences and other meetings, and Carey Moore and their dogs, Annabelle and Toby, make their home in Waxahachie, Texas, just south of Dallas.

To learn more about Pam, visit her website: www.moorelifelessons.net